For EVERYONE to Get Ahead and Live a Better Life...

Take Charge and Make It Happen!

Develop a Winning Attitude, Grow Yourself as an Exemplary Leader, and Succeed by Helping Others

Barnes Williamson

A *Possibility Press* Book

ISBN 978-0-938716-83-9

Published by *Possibility Press*
PossibilityPress.com

Manufactured in the United States of America

Dedicated to YOU!

May *Take Charge and Make It Happen!* help guide you in developing a stronger winning attitude, growing yourself as a leader, and succeeding by helping others.

May it help empower you take the actions necessary to realize your greatest aspirations and become the person you were created to be, while inspiring, encouraging, and helping others to do the same with what you have to share.

Contents

I credit much of my success to the guidance of those who believed in and encouraged me along the way.

So be sure to enlist the help of a leader who believes in and encourages you in growing yourself as a person and a leader.

Regardless of your financial situation, what you've achieved so far, your age, environment, ethnicity, or educational level, you can always elevate your thinking, take more productive action, and enrich your life.

Maintain a winning attitude, focus, determination, and commitment in making your vision of the future a reality.

Growing Through Tough Times...Molded for Leadership

"I don't run away from a challenge because I'm afraid. Instead, I run toward it because the only way to escape fear is to trample it beneath your feet." —Nadia Comaneci

CONFRONTED BY CHALLENGES, the only industry in the town where I grew up had to shut down, putting over half the men and women into the ranks of the unemployed. My father, who had struggled for years to buy a home for our growing family, was one of those who got laid off. As a result, we lost our home and moved into a rental a few miles away.

Fortunately, my dad was a dedicated, responsible, hardworking family man who always gave his best to everything he did. In addition to his full-time job he had been far-sighted enough to start and, with mom's help and us kids pitching in, run a home business, supplying a territory he had established in and around the nearby city.

As a result, after he lost his job my dad was able to continue providing for the family with his business income. While with several children it certainly wasn't easy, as my publisher says...

"When the going gets tough the weak blame someone or something else, and rarely take action or give up if they do. But leaders take charge and work diligently to make things happen!"

That was my dad's attitude. Undaunted, he just kept on going...no matter who or what got in his way!

Rich in Values, Commitment, and Action

Thankfully, my parents were strict disciplinarians who taught us to be honest, not only in dealing with others, but also with ourselves.

We weren't allowed to shirk responsibilities...especially to our family...and we were taught to have respect for authority and other people's property, ideas, and values. Whenever we were lacking in these areas, we were reminded by being disciplined

Feeling a strong responsibility to help the family I got a job, interrupting my education. Even though my grades were above average, I just felt it was the right thing to do. After leaving the service I re-enrolled in high school and, doubling-up on classes, got my diploma in a year.

This experience taught me that commitment and consistent action toward a worthwhile goal is essential for earning huge dividends. Of course, working smart is also key; otherwise, you could end up "spinning your wheels" like a hamster running inside a caged wheel... running fast but getting nowhere!

An Early Priceless Lesson in Leadership

After graduation, I worked for two years, saving enough money to go to a small business college. During my first semester I felt compelled to participate in student government.

Shortly after getting involved, however, I discovered I had a rather strong difference of opinion with a senior who had run things his way the previous year. We had different philosophies about what direction and impact the student body would have on the administration, and disagreed about each other's approach to leadership.

He was autocratic, insisting that only he had the best ideas and everything had to be done his way. But I was a participative leader who appreciated ideas from others and worked with and through them to accomplish goals.

"Carefrontation"—Confronting with Care

The result of our carefrontations was that we grew to understand and respect each other so much that we became close friends. A year later, I even asked him to be the best man at my wedding!

Challenges certainly provide opportunities for growth. For example, when you carefront someone concerning your feelings about their behavior and you do it in a non-attacking way, it establishes fertile ground for taking your relationship to a whole new level. The courage to carefront someone is worth the risk, otherwise the relationship usually stays stuck because of nonproductive behavioral patterns, often leading to its failure...as well as resentment.

A Budding Sales Leader

Because I needed the money, I bid for and received a contract to operate the college bookstore, relishing the responsibility. Fortunately, a large investment wasn't required because I didn't have any store rent to pay nor did I need any employees.

I was able to afford to stock the items I thought would sell and had full control over the operation. Since the store was located only five miles from a major supplier I didn't need to put much money into inventory. Having enjoyed sales in the bookstore, as well as in my building supply sales job just before college, I was convinced my future was in sales and sales leadership.

After graduating college, I became a rep with a major insurance company. Embracing it as my best chance to create the life I wanted, I worked hard and studied long hours. My income rose to levels I had never even dreamed of, reinforcing something I learned as a teenager: Honest, intelligent, relentless effort is always rewarded.

I did extremely well in the business because I had a dream for a great life, as well as a sense of mission and purpose, and quickly established a reputation for prompt reliable service. I also focused on gaining interpersonal skills, and understanding people and their wants and needs. Committed to excellence, I became a consummate student of the business, eagerly absorbing the training, developing myself, and putting the knowledge into practice to better serve my clients.

Develop Yourself and Cultivate an Even Stronger Work Ethic

As with all great businesses, the products and services our company offered improved over the years, requiring agents to keep learning. Whenever an older agent asked if I'd like to go back to when the product line was smaller and easier to understand, my response was always a resounding…"No way!" I welcomed changes as they benefited not only our customers but also my agents, the constant improvements enabling everyone to more readily succeed.

To grow and better serve its customers, a company must continually fine-tune, upgrade, and add to its product and service line. Likewise, to grow our career or business we must continually develop ourselves and our people skills, while increasing our knowledge and understanding of our profession. This winning approach will help you grow and improve your abilities, better enabling and empowering you to serve others and build your success. Continuing personal and professional growth is essential for continuing accomplishment.

Since stagnation steals success, keep growing and going while enjoying the process of following your mentor's or leader's recommendations. There's really no such thing as maintaining the status quo because things in life are always changing. You're either going backward or moving forward—stagnating and watching things happen, or growing and making things happen. So take charge and always be doing something proactive with your time toward accomplishing your dreams, goals, and objectives.

After investing four years in developing as an agent I advanced into leadership, growing that aspect of my life for the rest of my career. A big part of my success was based on the strong work ethic I, thankfully, was taught and developed as a child and teen. My actions as an agent and a leader of agents were always based on solid values and doing the right thing, finding great dignity and meaning in my work. I made mistakes, but always gave my best while maintaining integrity both with myself and those I served.

A Winning Attitude Is Required for Leadership Excellence

Having a winning attitude is central for reaching goals, as it affects your interactions with others and all you do.

As the new leader of an agency that was rated lowest in productivity among hundreds of agencies nationwide, I had a real challenge on my hands! My winning attitude and skills would be put to the test, as agents and unit managers looked to me for leadership. It wasn't a matter of getting my people to do as I said, but encouraging and coaching them to do as I did.

In addition to training and leading agents, I was also a working agent. Setting the example with an ambitious pace, I helped the agency rise above its pitiful standing by getting out there and pouring myself into meeting new people, building relationships, making presentations, sharing products … and bringing on new clients and agents! My productivity inspired everyone to get productively busy as well, pulling together as a team, and making things happen!

The foundational objective in helping my agents was to create an environment conducive to success. I made a commitment to increasing morale and upgrading their knowledge, empowering them to raise their self-esteem—the respect they feel for themselves—and boost their self-confidence, helping them stretch and grow to reach goals.

During the first year, we saw a 50 percent increase in productivity and a hefty income gain for my people, a result of helping them get what they wanted. When you help enough people you can get what you want! Support others in achieving their objectives, and you're more likely to make your own a reality.

Working together, we dug the agency out of its slump to rank in the top 20 percent nationally, and as high as an agency could rank regionally. Thankfully, we maintained that level for the rest of my career. I'm particularly gratified by the contributions my associates made to the financial security of their families, friends, and clients.

As you continue reaching out to others in your business or career, you're likely to also feel quite good about yourself, those with whom you're working and associating, and the clients or customers you're also serving. You'll find that the difference you're making in all those people's lives is personally gratifying, as well as professionally rewarding.

As a result of putting people first, our agency was extremely profitable for our company and agents, and beneficial for our policyholders. Everybody won! To maximize your potential for success, be sure to put people before products and services. Care about your associates and others you're helping, or could help, including... prospective customers, clients, and associates.

I credit much of my success to the guidance of those who believed in and encouraged me along the way. So be sure to enlist the help of a leader who believes in and encourages you in growing yourself as a person and a leader.

Regardless of your financial situation, what you've achieved so far, your age, environment, ethnicity, or educational level, you can always elevate your thinking, take more productive action, and enrich your life. Maintain a winning attitude, focus, determination, and commitment in making your vision of the future a reality.

Look at yourself, that fine person in the mirror, to move forward in turning your dreams and goals into accomplishments, while dreaming bigger than ever before. You're cast as the main character in the script of your life; yes, *you!* Go forward in faith in following your heartfelt dreams and you'll be on the right path...*for you.*

Keep reading and discover how powerful your attitude is in affecting your personal and business life, including your health, and in becoming more of a winner. Learn how to lead or be a more effective leader so you can better build your business or profession and realize your fondest aspirations. Now, more than ever, it's high time to *take charge and make it happen!* So let's get started...

How you shape your life is determined largely by your attitude.

With a proactive solution-oriented attitude you're taking charge. You're not at the mercy of the challenges you encounter in rising above your circumstances. You respond decisively, rather than feeling like a victim who believes you can't.

You immerse yourself in personal development—the grand life-long adventure of becoming the person you were created to be, living the life you dream of.

What could possibly be better than that?

—1—
How's Your Attitude?

"You can do anything you decide to do. What do dreams know of boundaries?" —Amelia Earhart

A WINNING ATTITUDE IS CENTRAL to all success, happiness, and meaning. It's reflected by your mood, thinking, feelings, and perspective, as shown by your facial expression, posture, tone of voice, words, and actions.

An Optimistic Outlook Offers Many Outstanding Advantages!

You're solution-oriented, a possibility thinker, and look for the good. With a winning attitude, you're wholeheartedly committed to achieving your goals and dreams, and more likely to meet winning-thinking people you can befriend, associate with, and serve.

You're on an upward spiral—life keeps getting better and better, and you're more likely to be happy, healthy, and successful in all areas. Your optimism will help you embrace the adventure of life, take winning actions, and make good things happen.

When it comes to success, there are three kinds of people:

1. Those who make things happen.
2. Those who watch things happen.
3. Those who wonder what happened.

Where do you fit in? Remember, it's never too late to change your attitude. If you have any remnants of a losing attitude, perhaps one that's been bogging you down for awhile, evict it from your mind now. Since no one else can change it for you, there's no point in waiting any longer. Tag, you're it! Adopting a winning outlook can help you make a breakthrough, that is, turn the tide, to take steps toward realizing new or even long-held dreams and goals.

Reject Losing Thoughts and Habits; Embrace Winning Ones!

You can establish new ways of thinking, as well as new habits, when you're serious about it and apply yourself. Focus on it. It takes only 21 days of practice to change a habit or develop a new one. Winning habits serve you and support your success. Losing habits hold you back and detract from your success.

If you find it necessary to change a habit of losing thinking into winning thinking, practice thinking winning thoughts for 21 days. Block any losing thoughts that threaten to enter your mind. Refuse to utter a pessimistic word or phrase; and immediately replace it with an optimistic idea related to your topic of conversation.

If you slip up, simply start over again with a new 21-day period. It's wonderful how we can change our habits and attitudes when our desire and commitment is strong enough! Habits and attitudes stem from our mental life. It need only take an instant to change your mind. Changing your mind leads to changing your life!

Like anything worthwhile, habit changes require effort; and even though you really want to make the change you may have to work diligently to make it happen. For example, successful people guard against losing ideas from ever getting into their minds by not watching, reading, or listening to negative news, hearsay, or gossip. You'd benefit by replacing any such disempowering habits by indulging yourself in reading empowering self-help books to help keep yourself motivated, growing, and developing winning habits.

You're helping yourself shift to a new set of habits and experiences. Associating with other forward-thinkers helps you to increase the winning thoughts entering your mind, while supporting you in gathering momentum in pursuing your dreams and goals. Patiently persevere as you transition from any old habits that may have been holding you back, to new habits that'll keep you moving on.

After practicing your new habits for awhile, you'll see, hear, and feel the winning changes taking place within you and notice them reflected in your life. You're letting go of the old and embracing the new. Persevere with a winning attitude and you'll eventually realize your goals and dreams, provided you stay on track, doing whatever it takes to hit your targets, resetting them as often as necessary.

People using average-thinking patterns don't even realize it. They're so entrenched in feeling like a victim that other average-thinking people give them sympathy or pity, thinking that might help. But this doesn't help! It only reinforces their weaknesses, as these are negative disempowering emotions.

Such people can be helped through empathy and understanding, along with mentoring by a leader who believes in, encourages, and empowers them to develop and use their strengths…so they can pull *themselves* out of the muck and mire of self-pity and move on in improving their lives. If they've been wallowing in the losing attitude of "misery loves company," wasting time commiserating with complainers, they need to let that go and embrace the winning attitude of…"success attracts success" and associating with winners.

Consider a weightlifter. Until they understand how weight training works and keep lifting heavier and heavier weights they can't keep growing stronger. Pity can't help them, but their coach can!

Now there are certain average-thinking people who, even though unhappy, have closed minds, refuse to change their thinking, and criticize or reject you. Unfortunately, there's not much you can do but wish them well and hope that they eventually see the light.

However, those with a sincere desire for change may even tell you so. Tell them they can do it, and recommend some books and audios that have helped you. Encourage them to make whatever changes are necessary to adopt and maintain a winning attitude so they can move forward too. Show them an excellent example and you could become an important role model in their lives.

The way you think evolves into the way you act or react. If you think losing thoughts and act in losing ways, losing results will follow as sure as night follows day. It's only when you think winning thoughts accompanied by winning actions, that winning results can follow! But even if results appear to be losing at first, with a winning attitude you'll discover the benefit in this so-called adversity. Just keep going and growing, looking for the good, no matter what.

If you think change can be challenging, you're right! You're also right if you think it's impossible … *unless* you change your thinking. You'll only change when the pain of staying the same is greater than the pain of changing. You can only rise to a new level by changing the thinking and actions that are keeping you stuck.

Are You Dwelling on the Problem or Focused on the Solution?

Of course, you need to think about what you're going to do before you do it. How you think about it determines what you'll do with it. Are you focused on just complaining about the problem, the so-called losing situation, or working toward creating a winning solution? Are you looking for excuses to avoid doing something, or are you looking for reasons to do something?

You can accomplish anything you set your mind to ... a new job, a promotion, a dream house, excellent health, more time with your family, a thriving business of your own, financial security, freedom, flexibility, travel, or whatever else you may want. Be a possibility thinker and put your mind to the task in a winning manner. Keep your focus on winning thoughts—on what you want to create in your life, rather than on what you don't want. You get what you focus on.

When I was a teenager, my dad told me, "If you think you can do something or if you think you can't do it, you're right." Our thinking is central to our success or lack of it. It's as simple as that.

How Do You Perceive Your Experiences?

You can view events in a winning or losing way, as good or as bad, depending on how you look at them. While you can't relive your life, you can choose to have a winning attitude about the past. How do you normally perceive your experiences? Do you give them a winning or a losing spin? Do you learn something to help you win as a result of what may appear to be a losing situation or circumstance? Remember the winning expressions ..."There's a silver lining behind every cloud," and "You can't have a rainbow without rain." Look for the good; be a good finder.

Here's an example: Would you agree that winning is generally believed to be the ultimate desired event? Did you know that losing, which is usually thought of as an undesirable event, could actually turn out to have a winning benefit?

Losing gives all of us a marvelous opportunity to learn from our mistakes—what doesn't work and what does. That, of course, is the winning side of losing. You strive to win, but as my dad told me years ago: "Regardless of whether you win or lose, it's more meaningful that you always be and do the best you can." Give it your all; keep going and growing.

As we go and grow through the ups and downs of life, working through and overcoming every challenge brings with it an equal or greater benefit. Always look for and embrace the benefit.

Do you want to enjoy every day and the wonders of life? Of course you do! Then turn every so-called losing experience into a winning one. Did the experience give you an unexpected chance to make a needed change? Did you learn something from it? Did you meet new people and develop new relationships? If you said yes to any of these questions, that qualifies a challenge as a winning event!

It always pays to be open-minded and look for the opportunity in every situation…no matter how it may at first appear to be.

Laughter Is the Best Medicine

Your attitude affects your health. For example, a losing attitude adversely impacts your health. It's even been reported that people with a losing attitude have a greater chance of premature death. Whereas when you have a winning attitude, you affect your health in a beneficial way.

Have you ever noticed that when you're upbeat you feel more energetic? When you think winning, uplifting thoughts that put a sparkle in your eye, a smile on your face, and a spring in your step, you're happy. How could that be anything but good for you?

Laughter may come easily for some, but most people don't laugh enough for their own good health. While illness isn't a laughing matter, perhaps it would help to poke fun at ourselves if we're not as well as we could be. Laughter is a form of mental jogging, as it moves internal organs, energizes, reduces stress, affirms life, and helps us deal with challenges. Lightness lifts us up; heaviness weighs us down. So let's be cheerful and lighthearted as shown in the movie *Patch Adams,* based on the incredible life story of Dr. Hunter Adams.

Laughter and winning feelings release endorphins. These are proteins that occur naturally in the brain and have potent pain relieving properties that can work wonders in healing an illness. Endorphins are natural painkillers and mood elevators. Laughter allows us, at least temporarily, to forget our ills and troubles. It increases our pulse and gives our respiratory system a workout.

In his book *Anatomy of an Illness*, from which a movie was made, Norman Cousins related that he had a serious, life-threatening disease. Since his prognosis was so poor, he realized his only hope for recovery lay within himself. He was convinced that, along with his doctor's guidance, a cheerful, fun-loving attitude, coupled with hope and faith, would help him recover and heal.

To prevent losing thoughts from entering his mind, Cousins' doctor agreed with his idea of getting away from any such inputs that might come from a hospital or home environment. So he isolated himself, renting a motel room where he viewed funny videos to help him laugh, be happy, and release endorphins.

His doctor was amazed when his disease went into remission. Living for many more years, he continued his research on how attitude affects health, becoming an adjunct professor in UCLA's

Department of Psychiatry and Biobehavioral Science for ten years, the only layperson on its faculty.

When you're well, laughter can help you stay well; if you aren't well, it can help you get well. It has a curative effect on emotions, body, and mind. Furthermore, it's contagious, allowing your family, friends, and associates to catch it, helping them fight their health and emotional problems as well.

Laughter can be used daily as a delightful cost-free therapy. Enjoy what you do and inject humor into your life as much as possible. Learn to laugh easily and don't take yourself too seriously. Most things you may be worried about, in the long run, are unlikely to happen. Worry doesn't solve anything; it only causes anxiety.

So do your best to put things into perspective. It'll help you be happier and healthier. Ask yourself, "Will this matter in five years?" Many situations aren't even worthy of thought next week let alone five years from now. With practice, we can become better and better at taking the challenges of life in stride. We can learn not to over analyze them and better control our attitude and emotional response. As a result, we'll have more energy to work through the situations, others will enjoy being around us more, and we'll be happier and probably more successful. It's definitely worth the effort.

The Power of Winning Attitudes

Later, Norman Cousins wrote an article for *Parade* magazine that really struck me. Titled "Hope Can Make You Well," segments of it are printed below with permission of *Parade* and Mrs. Cousins:

"The surgeon had actually seen the malignancy and couldn't get at it with his knife. He gave the young man a week, ten days at the most to live. He knew the nature of the cancer and its propensity to spread. Yet, after six years had gone by, something had kept it from spreading. What was the cause?

"This question has relevance not just for this young man, now twenty-four, but also for the thousands of cancer patients who have outlived the melancholy forecasts of the specialists. What most of these survivors have in common is their *attitude* toward their illness. These patients didn't dispute the diagnosis; they just defied the death verdict that went with it.

"Why does a blazing determination to live make a difference? Psychoneuroimmunology, a branch of medicine that deals with the interactions between the brain, its endocrine system, and the immune system, has produced some answers.

"Intense determination and hope, it's been discovered, can have a physiological effect. Studies have shown that winning feelings can actually stimulate the spleen, producing an increase in red blood cells and a corresponding increase in the number of cancer fighting cells. These cells can specifically destroy the cancer cells, one by one, leaving normal tissue untouched. This is unlike chemotherapy, which cannot distinguish between normal and malignant cells.

"That particular emotions can affect our bodies has been supported by various research projects. Harvard Medical School students were tested for immunoglobulins, which are a good index to the immune function, before and after viewing an amusing film. After laughter, there was a measurable increase in immunoglobulin.

"Such research is making obsolete the scientific notion that the central nervous system and the systems that control the immune and endocrine function are separate. All the winning forces—love, hope, faith, will to live, determination, purpose, festivity, and laughter—are powerful antagonists of depression. They help to create an environment that makes medical care more effective.

"It's nonsense to debate the usefulness of the body's healing forces versus the forces of medical science. With illness, the objective is to mobilize all the help you can get. The body's own healing system, coupled with appropriate medical treatment and diet, is the way to go to maximize the chances for success.

"The ability of the human body to turn back illness is one of the wonders of the world. Indeed, the more we know about the connection between mind and body, the greater the prospect that we can put it to work for our greater good."

Losing Attitudes Thwart Success and Can Even Make You Sick

It's widely understood that there's a mental-emotional link to many physical disorders, with a significant percentage of those who visit doctors suffering from illnesses caused by stress. If not overcome, anxiety, fear, anger, and distress not only negatively affect health and relationships, but also the ability to achieve our dreams and objectives.

Some people actually imagine themselves to be sick, suffering all the pain and anguish of the real thing, even though there's nothing physically wrong. By their thinking, their attitude, they create problematic symptoms. It's about what's "eating" them! Others are more predisposed, perhaps through family behavioral patterns or hereditary, to respond physically in certain ways to challenges. For example, they may have a family that, historically, has responded to stress by internalizing it and developing stomach ulcers.

The great news is anyone can eliminate any unhealthy thinking patterns they may have learned from the older generation. No one has to hold on to a losing mental state. We can all learn how to deal more effectively with various situations and overcome them.

No matter what happens to you, whether seemingly good or bad at the outset, your attitude definitely affects the outcome. Whenever you face overcoming a challenge in order to achieve a goal or dream, look at it as an opportunity to grow and achieve greater success.

How Might Your Job Situation Be Affecting Your Attitude?

Have you ever heard anyone say, "I'm sick and tired of my job," or felt that way yourself? If so, you're not alone, as surveys worldwide show 70-85% employee disengagement. The majority dislike (some even hate) their job or some aspect of it like…the pay, benefits, hours, environment, an unappreciative boss, or unhappy coworkers. Or perhaps they're bored, looking for a new challenge, or hoping for a transfer to a position they believe they'd like. Some even go back to school so they can advance their career or get into another field.

Also, due to the stressful frustrations of the commute—traffic, long lines, rude drivers, road rage, inclement weather—many workers suffer health issues like … neck pain, weight gain caused by eating fast food or sugary or salty snacks to get a "feel good" in their vehicle, as well as the expense and time lost on the road.

However, if it's an option, others are happier working for their employer from home, either as an employee or independent contractor. Still others like the extra income of an independent home business on the side, perhaps with the goal of gaining the flexibility and freedom that come from not being constrained by a job.

To have a winning attitude, it's vital to be engaged doing something that can enable you to create the life you want. The hope, alone, of achieving that can help you be healthier, happier, find more meaning in life, and even make a greater difference.

How Else Can We Avoid or Eliminate Any Losing Thinking?

- **Always think winning thoughts,** never worry or imagine something's wrong, and maintain the attitude that you can handle whatever comes your way. When you catch yourself thinking losing thoughts, stop and say, "I only think winning thoughts. I know I can make it happen; I'm committed to it!"

- **All work and no play is unhealthy**. Say you're working full-time, have a busy family, and even a business on the side. If you think you have no time for any fun activities, learn to blend them in with your business-related activities.

  For example, imagine you have an out-of-town job assignment or business function in a resort area. Perhaps you can bring your family along. You may want to take off an additional day or two to see some of the sites that are of interest, but only if it's financially wise to do so.

  Invite your sales staff or business associates to go dream-building with you, and meet some new people while you're at it. Look at beautiful properties or attend a car, boat, or builders show, or some other dream-reinforcing activity. You'll be getting to know your associates better, as well as building your dreams and theirs, while befriending new people. Take pictures and enjoy it.

  Some activities you now enjoy may need to be put on hold when you're chasing after a big goal and investing more of your time in that direction. You're having fun with the process of making your goals and dreams come true, while helping those around you maintain a winning attitude.

- **Rather than fretting over things you can't change,** devote your energy to the things you *can* change. Do it with a winning attitude, let go of any losing thoughts, look for the opportunity in the situation, and keep moving.

- **Include humor in your life** by telling funny stories about mistakes you've made, and encourage others to share such stories about themselves. Laugh, especially at yourself, whenever you get the chance. Look for the humor in everyday events and, as time goes on, you'll find it more easily. Have fun as you go about each day—lighten up and smile!

- **Be grateful for what you have.** Gratitude is a sure antidote for an ailing attitude. For example, if someone does something you don't like make a list of all the good they do. As your heart fills with gratitude it'll be easier to talk to them about your feelings concerning their behavior...and forgive them. Gratitude is key to happiness and joy—a simple, yet powerful trait to have and share.

- **Check with your family physician about exercising** regularly enough ... while raising your heart rate. It produces a natural high and helps relieve the distress and fear caused by losing thoughts. Combine your exercise with your daily routine and business activities. For example, at lunch you could listen to a motivational audio as you take a brisk walk.

- **Since your health is affected by your thinking,** think like a winner. Keep your mind on cheerful, happy thoughts and, once again, always be a good finder. As English clergyman and writer Charles Kingsley said, "Cheerfulness is full of significance; it suggests good health, a clear conscience, and a soul at peace with all human nature." So be a winner by using your energy to focus on and work toward your dreams. Just thinking about it is uplifting. You'll be happier and your body will thank you for it.

- **Accept responsibility for your actions,** and don't blame others for your challenges. Always look to yourself and ask, "What have I done to cause or contribute to the situation? How can I overcome it?" Your life is in *your* hands. As you continue moving on, be the captain of your ship, steering it in the direction of your dreams and goals...full speed ahead!

- **Make the decisions that affect your life;** don't delegate them to other people. Gather and carefully consider all the facts, and make an informed decision. Check with your mentor or leader for serious decisions affecting your job or business. Make the best decisions you can and keep going.

  Do your best to make your decisions work but, if necessary, alter your course of action. Be flexible, take it all in stride, and put it in perspective in terms of its importance in light of everything else in your life. Take action and keep moving. Life is a process.

- **Recognize any losing thoughts and events** that may creep into your life. Look for the perhaps "hidden" opportunities they present, and work through and learn from them.

- **Forgive yourself for the mistakes you make** and the weaknesses you need to overcome. Since having a forgiving nature is the foundation for caring about others, do your best to develop one no matter what others may say or do. Their behavior is about them and where they are attitudinally!

- **Since being with certain people is a negative experience,** you may only be able to care about them from a distance.

You could send them a positive message, wish them the best, or pray for them if so inclined. Hopefully, they'll respond positively to your kindness and change their attitude.

Love is a powerful winning emotion, and the world needs more of it! It starts with a caring attitude rather than making a situation worse by indulging, for example, in apathy. Care about others, encourage them to follow their dreams, big or small, and, whenever possible, create win-win relationships.

As Saint Mother Teresa shared ...*"Spread love everywhere you go. Let no one ever come to you without leaving happier."* You want others to be glad they met you!

- **Do as much good as you can on the job,** making it as pleasant an experience as possible. But if you find little meaning in what you do or you're not happy doing it, it may be time for a change. What would love to do and how could you earn the income that would enable you to do it?

  How about setting yourself up financially so you can have more time and money to do what you love to do? For example, you may want to have the resources so you can afford to offer your professional services for free whenever you want to...in your community and beyond.

  The key to knowing what you love to do is to ask yourself, "What would I do if time and money weren't of any concern?" Since doing the same thing over and over again, while expecting a different result could be considered insanity, do something that can enable you to get what you want.

Your Attitude Is Key to How You Shape Your Life!

As noted American psychologist William James revealed...

"The greatest discovery of my generation is that human beings can alter their lives by altering their attitudes of mind."

But what would motivate someone enough to alter their life? It takes a certain level of disenchantment with their situation coupled with the goal of accomplishing that. And since most people need to work anyway, why not work toward living a better life?

It requires little desire to live an ordinary lackluster life that includes indulging in non-productive distractions and escapes in an effort to cope with the monotony of working just to pay the bills. But who in their heart would honestly want to live like that?

Unfortunately, average ordinary lives are being lived by millions of dissatisfied people who may pretend all is well, but would like their lives to be better. Furthermore, all things and people are not as they appear to be, or as some would lead you to believe! But they're only deluding themselves by exhibiting a false image. They want to look successful before they've earned it, going in debt to keep up appearances, adding to their stress and unhappiness.

How you shape your life is determined largely by your attitude. With a proactive solution-oriented attitude you're taking charge. You're not at the mercy of the challenges you encounter in rising above your circumstances. You respond decisively, rather than feeling like a victim who believes you can't.

You immerse yourself in personal development—the grand lifelong adventure of becoming the person you were created to be, living the life you dream of. What could possibly be better than that?

As you pursue your dreams, goals, and objectives by reaching out to others, you're dedicated to increasing your awareness and knowledge of the principles of success and leadership, enabling you to fully live your purpose and make a difference! As author Helen Keller, the first deaf-blind person to earn a BA degree, realized...

> *"One can never consent to creep when one feels an impulse to soar. Life is either a grand adventure or nothing at all!"*

Carefully observe and analyze your attitudes. Are they beneficial or detrimental to your success and happiness? Consciously choose to accept or reject them based on whether they are helpful to achieving your goals. Be your own best friend, not your own worst enemy.

Twelve More Ideas to Help You Maintain a Winning Attitude

1. **Your success and happiness** depends primarily on your attitude!

2. **The purpose of your existence is not** to just make a living, but to make a life of valuable contributions with what you have to offer. It's through your job, business, and personal life that you make a difference in the lives of others, as well as in your own.

3. **A losing thought** is an investment in a commitment to fail.

4. **While you may regret something you did,** you're more likely to regret something you could have done but didn't. Claim your power and take action with what you know, or discover, that you need to do to reach your goals. Ask yourself, "If not now, then when? If not this, then what?" Don't let anyone or anything stop you from doing what's necessary to make it happen!

5. **Only those with a self-responsibility attitude** can turn their wishes into dreams, dreams into goals, and goals into reality. Complaining doesn't get anything done; and those who take the stance of a victim and blame others or circumstances can never win. Relying on someone or something else to make them successful doesn't work either!
6. **The ultimate cost of something is time** ... the amount of your life that you exchange for it.
7. **Youthful exuberance is an attitude**; it's not just reserved for a certain time of life. You can crank it up any time you wish!
8. **Those who haven't yet determined their purpose** in life or aren't yet working toward its fulfillment are easy prey for anxiety. They're like a ship without a rudder—yielding to the force and direction of the wind and the waves—being bashed and battered about, trying to just stay afloat, not getting anywhere.
9. **Be enthusiastic.** The worst bankruptcy is the person who has lost enthusiasm.
10. **It's not the nature of the situation that matters.** It's your attitude and response toward it. Defeat it or let it defeat you.
11. **"Most of the shadows in life are caused by** standing in one's own sunshine."—Ralph Waldo Emerson
12. **No one can make you feel mediocre** unless you let them. Your attitude about yourself is up to you. So choose a winning one!

Go with What You've Got, Right Where You Are!

Fear and anxiety cause stress that can have a debilitating effect on your mind, body, and spirit. Replace them with the ingredients of a winning attitude, including such virtues as—faith, belief, integrity, responsibility, trust, optimism, common sense, empathy, diplomacy, graciousness, open-mindedness, unselfish giving, courage, gratitude, self-motivation, and hope.

Cultivate and employ those ingredients as you take charge and make it happen. Sincerely want to win and take appropriate action, while emulating excellent leaders who have incorporated them into the fabric of their lives. You don't have to know everything, and there's no convenient time. Success isn't built on everything being perfect. Go with what you've got, right where you are. Do it now!

Stress can be beneficial. Without any you'd have a boring ordinary existence!

Stress can stimulate you to greater achievement, enabling you to get ahead and create a better life.

Managing stress is vital for developing a healthier happier more successful life with greater purpose and meaning. How stress affects you depends on your attitude toward it.

Purge any beliefs about stress that are detrimental to you and your objectives, and it will be easier to make it work for rather than against you.

—2—

How Do You Let Stress Affect Your Attitude?

"The greater the challenge the greater the victory! What we obtain too cheaply we esteem too lightly; 'tis dearness only that gives everything its value." —Thomas Paine

THE DICTIONARY DEFINES "STRESS" AS—"pressure, strain, a force that tends to distort a body; intense effort; a factor that induces bodily or mental tension; also a state induced by such stress."

How are you feeling about how things are going for you? You develop your attitudes and feelings based on your past experiences, your perception of them, and what you have learned from them, coupled with your view of reality in general.

- Winning feelings include love, gratitude, forgiveness, trust, compassion, respect, admiration, and such.
- Losing feelings include hate, distrust, anger, jealousy, resentment, fear, self-pity, and the like.
- Indifferent feelings reflect an "I-don't-care-whatever" attitude; an ambivalent, noncommittal "straddling of the fence."

Which of these feelings do you predominantly hold within you? The most influential factor governing your behavior is how you feel—which arises from your thinking—that is, your attitude. Your peace of mind or anxieties, security or insecurity, fulfillment or frustration, success or failure, happiness or sadness all stem from your attitudes and feelings. Understanding these feelings and attitudes is essential in preparing yourself to control stress.

It's impossible to avoid all stress. For example, you experience stress whenever you do something you don't like or enjoy. It could be driving in traffic, especially to a job you don't like, running late for something, working with average-thinking people, and financial challenges. Fortunately, you can set your life up to do more of what you enjoy, which may be one reason you're reading this book.

Creating more of the life you want, thus reducing your stress in certain areas is part of the answer. It's also important that you learn to manage stress. Controlled and managed stress is beneficial, because that's part of what drives you toward your goals. Top-notch leaders have learned to manage stress. Failing to do so can lead to a losing attitude, loss of self-esteem and self-confidence, difficulty in reaching goals, and poor health.

Do You Have a Particularly Stressful Job?

Stress on the job is common. Some people have tight deadlines, like those involved in producing a product or providing a service that's in high demand. Perhaps they feel that they're not given adequate time to do a thorough enough job that meets their standards of excellence.

Others may feel overworked, or without proper guidance, left to fend for themselves on their assignments. They may have bosses who manage by intimidation or fail to recognize their contributions. Or they may be unclear about the various levels of responsibility. As time goes by, especially as they continue to grow and develop, these deficiencies will become more glaring and need to be addressed.

At some point in your career you may have noticed others being promoted to positions for which they're not even close to being ready for. They may have been compliant "yes" people or friends or relatives of the owner. Or perhaps a newly appointed person was given more responsibility than they were prepared to handle. These and many other difficulties can contribute to stress on the job.

Is Your Stress Controlled or Uncontrolled?

Stress has been around forever. However, it's only since the industrial revolution that doctors and scientists have studied it to learn what effects stress may have on the mind and body. Uncontrolled chronic stress can lead to heart disease and sudden cardiac death. Controlled stress, however, can lead to a more productive and happier, but also a healthier, longer, and more significant life. What kind of stress are you under; controlled or uncontrolled?

The medical community recognizes seven risk factors directly responsible for heart disease:

- High blood pressure
- Overweight
- Diabetes
- Smoking
- High cholesterol
- Family history
- Chronic Stress

Of the seven, the only one you can't control is family history. All of the others, however, can be controlled when you decide it's imperative to your health...mental, physical, and emotional. Be sure to consult with your doctor for advice and support on this.

A Winning Attitude Toward Stress Is Necessary for Success

Stress can be beneficial. Without any at all you'd have a boring ordinary existence! Stress can stimulate you to greater achievement, enabling you to get ahead and create a better life. Managing stress is vital for developing a healthier happier more successful life with greater purpose and meaning.

How stress affects you depends on your attitude toward it which, fortunately, is under your control. Purge any beliefs about stress that are detrimental to you and your objectives, and it will be easier to make it work for you as a motivator, rather than against you as a deterrent.

Since situations can be perceived differently, what some people consider stressful can be challenging and motivating to others. What's makes the difference? It's about controlling your attitude toward stress. It helps to always look for the redeeming aspects of what may, at first, appear to be an adverse situation. However, adversity can be our greatest teacher, provided we're open to learning from and growing through it.

As leading Roman lyric poet Horace shared...

"Adversity has the effect of eliciting talents, which in prosperous circumstances would have lain dormant."

Self-Esteem Is Necessary to More Effectively Deal with Stress

People who manage stress without experiencing its ill affects are able to do so largely because of self-esteem, which enables them to be more in control of themselves and their own well-being.

They're deeply committed to and excited about their purpose and what they need to do to make things happen. They understand the value of embracing the challenges of overcoming obstacles while helping others, setting the example of striving, developing themselves, and growing as a leader.

They create win-win situations, as win-lose and lose-win are simply not options. While not taking themselves too seriously, they do take their responsibilities as contributing members of society seriously, considering the process a great quest. Unlike average-thinking people who let challenges stymie them, win-win creators establish the habit of hurdling over obstacles, taking challenges in stride.

One such business-owner friend of mine shared how he had handled someone who was demonstrating a rather demanding, overbearing attitude. While my friend had been dealing effectively with this feisty client for years, this situation was totally unacceptable, requiring a more assertive approach. My friend's attitude in dealing with this type of personality was that, "No one can rattle my cage (upset my peace of mind) because I don't have a cage to rattle!"

My friend explained that he had just gotten off the phone with the client who, at the beginning of the conversation threatened, "I'm going to ruin your day!" To which he replied, "No you're not! I'm not giving you permission. Now what can I do to help you?"

A person with healthy self-esteem knows they're in charge of their own attitude in responding to challenging people and situations, and will not allow anyone to stress them out. Lack of self-esteem is a serious source of stress, the root cause of the inability of countless people to handle stress effectively. Why? They simply don't have the courage to speak up for themselves and, therefore, become "doormats," habitually allowing others to take unfair advantage of them. The more they let that happen, the more stress they experience.

Identifying a Shortage of Self-Esteem and Then Bolstering It

How can you identify a lack of self-esteem? It's often characterized by low self-confidence, shyness, fear, anxiety, anger, resentment, and inappropriate people-pleasing tendencies. Self-esteem begins with the family environment and it's a product of life's influences and our responses to them, which will be explored in more detail in Chapter 10. It can be raised or lowered, often depending on one's exposure to winning or losing attitudes and how the individual allows themselves to be influenced by others, generally without even realizing it.

Some kids grow up in an environment where they're often put down and ridiculed by those who are important to them and supposedly love them. However, there may be a ray of hope in their life ... a neighbor, supportive teacher, guidance counselor, coach, pastor, a community center leader, or someone else who believes in, affirms, and encourages them to go for their dream. That person keeps rallying for the child to succeed and never gives up on them, thereby helping build their self-esteem.

After the student graduates from high school, they keep in touch with the encourager. Now in college, they find another individual who cheers them on, or they may even continue being mentored long-distance by their original encourager.

Some think that once a person's self-esteem is beaten up it's forever destroyed. But that's true only if they never find mentoring or encouragement that can help them rise from the ashes of their negative upbringing. While having a real live mentor or encourager would be best for most people, "mentoring" can actually begin and be furthered by reading personal development book(s).

Anyone who's earnest and has a strong enough desire *can* find such a person or book(s), ideally both, which is key to growing self-esteem. It could be a leader who sees past insecurities and unskillful behavior, recognizes strengths and potential, recommends and encourage reading personal development books, and inspires them to move forward...by taking inspiring actions themselves!

So how's your self-esteem? How do you feel about yourself? Hint...this is reflected in how you behave toward others. Are you quick to find fault? Do you easily criticize? Do you have difficulty showing love and affection? If you have any of these weaknesses as you interact with others, take notice that this is also how you treat yourself. It all starts with you. Do you respect yourself enough to do what it takes to create the life you want to live?

Healthy self-esteem is based on humility and recognizes the shortcomings we need to grow beyond ... so we can better lead and serve. No one is "perfect," even though some may think they are; that's ego-based arrogance. However, those with healthy self-esteem accept responsibility and rectify any losing ways.

Do you have any behaviors that are hindering your success? If you feel alone here, rest assured everyone has some habits that could be eliminated or improved upon. Don't let anyone fool you! Start by writing a list of habits you'd like to change. Then identify the one that's holding you back the most from achieving your goals,

and work toward changing that behavior first. It can be challenging, but it's essential for you change what you're currently doing that isn't giving you the results you want.

So, do you have a mentor...someone who believes in you? Is there a leader in your industry who you can relate to, perhaps with a similar background? Is someone available to encourage you to grow as a leader? Is there a leader from whom you could learn more about becoming a leader yourself, so you can assist others in growing and pursuing *their* objectives?

Recognize the winner in you and see yourself as a strong, yet compassionate, leader with healthy self-esteem, easily able to deal with stress. All such leaders had to change their thinking and behaviors in certain areas in order to become better role models and lead more effectively. Do likewise and you, too, can excel in supporting others in doing the same, realizing great satisfaction in helping them succeed. The more people you help the more you can get ahead.

Your life can be more fulfilling and enjoyable, no matter how developed you already may be. We all have more potential than we probably realize. As each new behavior you adopt becomes a habit, go back to the list and choose another behavior to change. If necessary, ask for help from someone who cares about you.

When you believe you're finished with the list, ask yourself if there are still any other behaviors that need changing. Keep growing and becoming the best you can be every day of your life. As former US President Theodore Roosevelt said, "Do what you can with what you have, right where you are."

Here's a contemporary version of an excerpt from *The Autobiography of Benjamin Franklin* where he shared his approach to changing behaviors. This can help you make the changes necessary to build your self-esteem and more effectively deal with stress. As Franklin did, take it step by step and you'll find it more doable...

> *"I intend to adopt all of these virtues—temperance, silence, order, resolution, frugality, industry, sincerity, justice, moderation, cleanliness, tranquility, chastity, and humility. However, I've decided that I wouldn't strive to acquire all these qualities at one time. As I master each one, I'll go on to master the next quality etc., until I've developed all 13...."*

A Winning Attitude Helps You Live Stronger and Longer

As discussed, endorphins are triggered by exercising at an increased heart rate. Known as a natural healer, they're also produced by the brain through having a winning attitude and laughing. It's been observed that people with winning attitudes tend to live stronger and longer than those with losing attitudes.

At the opposite end of the spectrum, catecholamine, chemicals released throughout the body by excessive stress, can damage blood vessels and arteries. While it may take years before the damage is severe enough to affect your health, your arteries and heart can take only so much abuse before they react and cause serious coronary damage. A sudden stressful situation can trigger an immediate realization that something is wrong.

Beware of losing thoughts. Those who allow themselves to be programmed by them, whether they realize it or not, go on to develop losing attitudes that lead to making poor choices, causing themselves to become prime targets for stress-related health problems. Fortunately, focusing on objectives, coupled with a winning attitude and enthusiasm and being around positive people, nurtures self-esteem, confidence, determination, and high self-expectations, all of which are deterrents to those problems.

Another key to developing a winning attitude, thereby reducing stress, is to always be learning and increasing your optimism, personally and professionally. It energizes your thinking to eliminate and replace any losing thoughts you may have with winning ones. It can be as simple as reading personal development books rather than novels, listening to empowering audios rather than uninspiring music, and attending motivational seminars and webinars rather than disempowering movies. It's all about adopting winning habits.

Book Readers Can Live Longer and Earn Higher Incomes!

A recent study done at Yale School of Public Health found that people who read at least 30 minutes a day for several years lived an average of two years longer than those who didn't read at all, and had higher incomes. Also, Guglielmo Weber, Prof. of Econometrics and a researcher at the University of Padua, found that children who grew up with books earn more money as adults, and said that...

"In this sense we claim books, like diamonds, are forever."

A winning attitude fills you with enthusiasm and anticipation; whereas a losing attitude drains and discourages you. It's easy to believe in the power of a winning focus to enhance your physical, mental, emotional, and financial well-being, isn't it? The evidence of its benefits is widely recognized by the medical community.

What Causes Stress?

The underlying cause of stress is usually the belief that we're not in control of our life, which is really ourselves. To one degree or another many falsely perceive themselves as just victims of circumstance. The amount of stress experienced generally relates to the amount of control the individual has "lost" over their life which, in reality, they've given to others in one way or another.

Stress can be caused by the perception of a threat, either physically or emotionally. It could be the fear of losing a job, of not being able to pay the bills, or some other concern. Fear comes from worrying that we may not be able to handle whatever comes our way. Developing the faith and confidence that, perhaps with help, we can handle anything we're faced with is the main stress eliminator. It behooves all of us to be alert and strive to develop and maintain this attitude.

What Are the Warning Signs?

Fortunately, there are stress warning signs that tell you something's wrong. However, they're not the same for everyone. Reactions to circumstances differ from person to person due to the influence of environments, experiences, relationships, and attitudes.

Some of the physical warning signs include: frequent indigestion, tightness in the neck and/or shoulder muscles, frequent headaches, difficulty sleeping, and a racing heartbeat. Some emotional warning signs include: fear, anxiety, anger, resentment, and distress about what is happening in your life.

How Can Stress Be Managed Effectively?

Managing stress is essential for our health, but also so we can maintain self-control and rational behavior. Healthy stress management leads to an even greater sense of control. It can also cause a chain of winning events to occur, which you can think of as a reward for managing your stress!

In the process, you may need to learn to identify oncoming stress, which will help you ward against a losing pattern...by interrupting it. Cut it off at the pass, so to speak, with a winning attitude and taking positive action. This is key in helping you gain momentum toward handling stress effectively.

You have the power to control your emotions. No one has that power over you, unless you give it to them. Likewise, no one can ruin your day, your attitude, unless you let them.

Things happen, and they can usually be interpreted in a number of ways. Through your thinking, you filter the event based on your own perspective. Depending on your attitude, you'll feel certain emotions. If you perceived the event as a negative, that nothing good can come of it, you'll feel stressed about it. However, interpret the event an opportunity to win, or something that can be turned into one, and you won't be stressed… even if it presents a challenge!

A simple example is a rainstorm. If you're a farmer and you've just been through a long drought, you'd be mighty happy to finally see some rain. On the other hand, if you were on vacation and had planned to go swimming in the ocean that day, you'd probably be disappointed, at least at first. So how do you manage your thinking so that a momentary feeling of disappointment doesn't grow into a daylong losing attitude that would affect you and others? First you'd accept the fact that you can't change the weather and then relax with it—let go of the tension in your body. Then you would look for something else pleasant to do, perhaps indoors, that you would enjoy as much or maybe even more. Look for the good in everything and everyone. As Dale Carnegie put it…

> *"Remember, happiness doesn't depend upon who you are or what you have; it depends solely upon what you think."*

Go for excellence, but don't expect perfection…from either yourself or others! Remember, nobody's perfect. People with perfectionistic attitudes are more prone to stress… unless and until they become flexible. Such people need to let go of the idea that their way is the only way. They also need to delegate—allow other people to get things done—even though the other person's approach may be different in striving for the same basic result.

Adopt the attitude that you'll go for the results you want with all your heart, but you're unattached to the outcome. You won't let yourself get upset even if the worst thing, in your opinion, that could happen does happen. No matter the results, getting all riled up would only make matters worse. Know you can handle it. That way you'll be as prepared as possible for the consequences…without stress. Strive to do your best and you'll often get excellence along the way. Even if you don't, though, you can rest with the fact that you gave it your best. What more can anyone do? Better your best!

To manage stress effectively, first determine its cause. Write down what or who you believe is stressful. Take each one and think what you can do to reduce, change, or eliminate what's causing the stress. Perhaps you could do so with the support of your family, friends, boss, leader, or mentor. You may be surprised how much you really *can* do, even in small ways, when you're committed to it. However, you'll be in a better position to make that determination by reviewing the list, and then taking appropriate action!

Say you're building your business or profession to gain more freedom, flexibility, and control over your life, while juggling other responsibilities. A great technique for managing stress is to list the things you need or want to accomplish each day or week, separating them into two categories, as follows:

> **Category One—What you need to do but don't like or are hesitant to do.** Maybe you've been putting off calling people on your prospective associate and customer lists. Even if you're afraid, do it anyway... and watch what happens. We grow the most when we do the things we fear the most, and as we do the fear goes away. The things we fear doing the most are the things we need to do the most. Have you ever noticed that?
>
> Attack the first category with determination and gusto. You may be surprised how easy it is to do those things once you take the first step and get moving. Getting started is the hardest part. Once you gain momentum, the rest can go almost automatically. Then go to the second category.
>
> **Category Two—What you need to do and like to do.** By doing only what you like to do first, which is how many people operate, you'll experience unnecessary stress. The unhappy anticipation of doing what you don't enjoy or are afraid to do may be worse than just getting those things done and out of the way.
>
> You'll be more relaxed, and have less stress ... both in the short- and long-run ... by first accomplishing Category-One tasks. While you're doing them, you can look forward to doing what you like to do as a reward for completing them. Anticipating doing what you like can be a great joy!

Change What You Can

Alcoholics Anonymous uses a wonderful prayer to help people sort things out: "God grant me the serenity to accept the things I cannot change, the courage to change the things I can, and the wisdom to know the difference."

For things you can change, list what and how the changes can be made, decide when they will be made...and then do it! Procrastination not allowed. Take high stress items first and work down the list. For example, you may have a number of so-called friends who have been somewhat negative toward you since you began seriously building your career or business in following your cherished goals and dreams. So start associating with more winning-thinking individuals who are doing the same. Put this on your list.

The best way to move forward in your quest for a better life is to focus on and be drawn by your dreams, goals, and objectives. Having dreams that may seem impossible or implausible without help will cause you to reach out to others, stretching and growing as you strive to make them your new reality. As they're accomplishing things, many leaders will tell you that they challenge themselves to continually dream ever bigger dreams, which helps keep them motivated.

Yes, have "impossible" dreams—something grand to go for—breaking them down into workable goals, so they're step-by-step attainable. Big goals are, quite simply, dreams with dates on them. If they turn out to be unreachable within the time frame you've set, reset them, which helps keep your hope alive, reducing your stress. Your leader or mentor can encourage and help you with this.

Keep resetting your goals, as often as necessary, until you accomplish them. That's what winners do; they persist until they make it happen. Be optimistic as to what you can do in a given period of time, considering all the priorities you may be juggling. You may need to eliminate some less productive activities, at least for now.

What Behavioral Patterns Are Best for Leadership Success?

Whenever success is discussed, the term Type A often enters the conversation. So what are the behavioral patterns of Type A and how do they relate to stress? Are there any detrimental consequences to being a Type A? What about a Type B? How do the two differ? Is one better than the other? Or could a mix and modification of certain of the characteristics be more appropriate for health and happiness, as well as success in leadership?

Type A's tend to be outgoing, have a sense of urgency, take charge, and are ambitious, proactive, competitive, and tenacious. They also have a strong desire for and love achieving, while being relentless in their pursuit of making it happen—all qualities of great leaders. But if they let their position or accomplishments lead to a big ego and grow impatient and aggressive, they'll lack empathy, which can lead to fault-finding, conflict, hostility, and stress.

Rather than developing and maintaining the fine relationships necessary for true success and happiness, people with big egos are likely to alienate and repel others. After all, who wants to be around a difficult-to-deal-with person? Their intensity, especially if they become hostile, is stressful not only for others, but also for themselves; and since no one can get away from themselves, those exhibiting it are often adversely affected the most.

While an achievement orientation is essential for successful leadership, doing so with hostility and aggression, while failing to show any positive emotion, could lead to high blood pressure and coronary artery disease ... the cause of most heart attacks. Unfortunately, it sometimes takes a serious life-threatening event to "wake up" people who exhibit those behaviors as to what they're doing to themselves, as well as to others, health-wise and otherwise.

These people would do well by being confident in relating with others, that is, caring about, empowering, and encouraging them instead of being bossy, making demands, and trying to control them. Otherwise, they're likely to overwhelm, and perhaps intimidate others like ... prospects, customers, clients, associates, friends, family members and anyone else with whom they come in contact. They would also do well by expressing their thoughts and feelings with empathy and understanding, as people not only like to, but also need to, be around people who care about them!

Those exhibiting Type B behavior tend to be introverted, noncompetitive, content, peaceful, patient, flexible and thoughtful, humble, gracious, creative and imaginative; and they also look for the good in others, while being steady workers. In addition, they tend to focus on one thing at a time, preferring to enjoy the process, and generally are less stressed than those exhibiting Type A behavior. While they may like to accomplish things, and many people with these traits can be very successful, they're less likely to be stressed if they don't achieve what they want and/or when they want it.

But in order to get ahead it's vital to be aware that "time is marching on"... or you'll never get anywhere! You realize that you don't want your life to go by without having achieved your dreams, goals, and objectives, while finding more meaning and making a greater difference. You're making your career or business a priority ... considering it a vital part of your life. While being overwrought about moving forward would be harmful to your health and well-being, it's essential to have a healthy sense of urgency and importance about what you're doing.

When you realize how fortunate you are to be in the business or career you've chosen, you'll appreciate the importance of being committed in doing whatever it takes to realize your aspirations through it. You've probably already noticed that life without proactively working toward your dreams and goals is empty and stressful. How could working a job, perhaps barely getting through the day, just to earn enough income to pay bills lead to anything but mediocrity, disappointment, and mounting stress?

Excellent leaders exhibit a blend of the best of Type A and B behaviors, are good examples of health and strength, and considerate of how they treat others, knowing everyone has challenges to deal with. For example, when leaders are out and about they extend the hand of friendship in meeting new people and kindly encourage them, lifting their spirits. They pay attention to the other person's wants and needs, honestly caring about them and their well-being.

As some leaders say, "You can't push a rope, but you can gently pull a wet noodle." So treat people as if they were wet noodles (sensitive) that can be gently pulled (led) and you won't alienate them. Always be considerate of others; never pushy.

What about Anger and Resentment?

Even though they're often mistaken as the same thing, anger and resentment are different. Anger is a strong feeling of annoyance or displeasure that can be aroused by someone or something you don't like, or something that's not producing the results you want or not going like you thought it would.

Resentment evolves out of anger when someone constantly blames instead of taking responsibility for their role in whatever happens that they didn't like. In doing so, they allow anger to simmer or persist, perhaps even to the point of imagining revenge. As some people would describe it, it's like having "a chip on your shoulder," defined in *The Dictionary of Clichés* as—"to be edgy, snappish; ready to fight." It's being antagonistic with a feeling of opposition and resistance to others' thoughts, feelings, and actions.

If you're angry or afraid, anger being based on the fear of a genuine or believed threat, and focus on it, you'll increase your stress. Since whatever you focus on expands its presence, focusing on winning leads to more winning. But if your focus is fear- or anger-based it can lead to harmful results health-wise, as such feelings can cause blood pressure and pulse to dramatically increase. This focus can also harm your relationships, generating even more stress.

The great news is that if you do feel angry or afraid, you can adjust your attitude. Take some deep breaths and refocus. Shift your thinking to something positive like pleasant sounds. This may include waves gently breaking in the surf, soothing music, or the sounds of nature. Relaxing activity can reduce blood pressure and slow your pulse, reducing your level of stress.

When someone has been personally and professionally developing themselves and has resolved various issues of their life while ridding themselves of any anger, nothing can upset them, at least not for very long. You could think of it like this: When you squeeze a lemon, sour lemon juice comes out. But when you squeeze an orange, sweet orange juice comes out.

An angry person is like a lemon. As long as they retain their anger, when they're pressured the only thing that can come out of them is sour. They would do well to let go of any pride they may have that contributed to creating the aggravating situation. Then they could choose a winning solution-oriented attitude about it all, and do whatever is in their power to remedy it. This could contribute to their angry attitude softening, to the point where they want to work things out, acknowledging their part in the matter, apologizing as appropriate. No matter what transpires as a result, though, they need to look for the good and what they've learned from it all...in essence making lemonade out of lemon juice.

Be Forgiving

Forgiveness helps diffuse and eliminate anger and resentment. It doesn't mean to forget or condone someone else's unskillful behavior; you need to remember it in order to forgive. You may or may not choose, or even be able, to communicate your forgiveness to the other person, especially if they've passed away. Forgive for your own well-being, as well as that of others.

Why is forgiveness so essential for successful leadership? The quality of your relationships will suffer if you're not forgiving. Forgiveness frees you from any losing grip the past may have had on you; it's an energizing, liberating, healing experience that helps you move on. Forgiveness is a beautiful demonstration of an attitude that says, "I care about you and value our relationship." Forgiveness may well be necessary before it's possible to have the cooperation of others that can lead to success, happiness, and a more meaningful life.

Be Appreciative

Another key to adjusting your attitude and letting go of anger and resentment is to adopt an attitude of appreciation. For example, it's easier to be positive when you take an honest look at all the good you already have in your life, as well as all the good the person who offended you has done.

Write them a letter expressing your thankfulness for whatever they've done that's made a positive difference in your life. You can choose to send it or not. Either way, going through this process helps you to get the challenge in perspective and melt away your anger.

As you've undoubtedly noticed, we're living in a world of people who often exhibit unskilled behavior. All of us need to deal with this reality and know that our behavior isn't always skilled either, as much as we may not want to admit it! In a majority of situations, both parties contributed in some way to the challenge at hand. There may have been a lack of clear communication, leading to a misunderstanding, which is often the case.

Acknowledge and Accept Responsibility

One of the most effective stress relievers is to take responsibility for your part of the situation and readily admit you made a mistake, which often diffuses it. Being defensive only escalates the high-volume discussion and thwarts resolution of the disagreement. Beyond taking responsibility for our role in the situation, we need to focus our comments on the behavior of the person(s) we're dealing with. Labeling and name-calling will only antagonize them.

For example, after Roy had been in business for a year or so, his neighbor friend, Tony, started noticing that he always seemed to be upbeat. "Sounds like things are going well for you. I only wish I could say the same. Did you get a promotion or something?"

"Tony, as you may recall, last year you said you weren't very happy with your job or income, which is how I used to feel. I told you that to get ahead I was building my own business on the side. But you grumbled you were too busy, so I just forgot about it!"

"Oh," Tony lamented. "I wish I had asked you to show me what you were doing, as things at work have only gotten worse."

"I'm sorry, Tony, that I didn't encourage you to, at least, sit down with me for a couple minutes so I could go over it with you."

Being a forgiving soul, Tony said, "That's okay. I just thought things would get better, and now realize I've got to *do* something!"

The point is, as situations arise take responsibility by addressing, working through, learning from, and resolving them in a respectful manner. Be sure to let go of any lingering losing feelings and move on. Holding on to anger and resentment, as in not forgiving, claims valuable energy, and keeps you stuck. Peace of mind is attained as we admit our mistakes, forgive others and ourselves, and persistently create win-win situations in all areas of our lives.

You may be feeling angry and resentful toward others who never seem to understand what you're striving to achieve in your career or business. They may have given up on their dreams years ago, referring to them as a joke or as "pie in the sky." They might even be referring to your dreams as farfetched, probably full of self-doubt and envy.

Associate with Like-Minded People

As you move forward in doing what's right for you and your family, you may find it necessary to limit your relationships with certain people in your life who, no matter what you say or do, are impossible to reason with. This could include those who are putting you or what you're doing down, perhaps even trying to hold you back with their negative losing attitude, casting aspersions.

While transitioning like this may, at first, be uncomfortable, it's part of your commitment in developing yourself, while following your path and finding like-minded people with whom you can beneficially associate. You want to be around those who are available to encourage, guide, or help you in your quest to get ahead or whatever else you're striving for. Seek them out and emulate the leaders.

Impatience Verses Enthusiasm

People exhibiting Type A behavior often mistake impatience for enthusiasm. They seem to believe aggressive behavior will bring them quicker, greater success. Instead, it impedes progress as it hurts relationships, making others disinclined to want to cooperate or work with them, or even quit; and they're more likely to make mistakes task-wise. Whereas, people exhibiting Type B behavior invariably are more patient, and enjoy more harmonious relationships with their families, associates, leaders, friends, and others.

Now you might be saying to yourself, "Oh my, I've been exhibiting certain less-than-desirable behaviors for years." If so, forgive yourself! All of us, no matter how "together" we may appear to be, have done things that, in retrospect, after growing and gaining wisdom, we'd certainly do differently. So you're definitely not alone.

The good news is, each moment is a new beginning, and we can all change our thinking and behavior to be more like the person we'd like to be. This helps us to go forward and achieve a new success. No one has to stay the same if it isn't serving them. We can all grow and change… and move on in whatever areas we want to. It simply starts with making different choices.

More Ideas for Reducing Stress

While opportunity is found in change, it can be accompanied by stress. Everything is subject to change, and we all need to be flexible in handling it to minimize or eliminate the stress we experience. Fortunately, by adopting a new attitude we can even eliminate the stress altogether. When we put our hearts and souls into it, have faith that it'll all turn out for the best, and we're unattached to the outcome, our stress can disappear.

Time/activity management, discussed in a following chapter, is another method you can use to cope with stress. You can be confident knowing you have the time to do those things that you need to do. Perhaps you can delegate some tasks others can do and still be able to do those things that are not as crucial toward reaching your goal, but are still important to you.

Without effective time/activity management people often "spin their wheels," accomplishing little, if anything at all. They flounder around by doing "category two"—often-unimportant maintenance tasks that have little or no effect on their goal accomplishment. The result is that they get backed up on the tasks that *are* important to achieving their goals. Then they wonder why they aren't making any progress. Unfortunately, few of them look to themselves as the cause of their lack of success! Instead, they come up with some incredible excuses.

Surround yourself with people you like who are positive, upbeat, and ambitious. Since nearly everyone needs to earn a living, it's certainly more enjoyable, rewarding, and less stressful to work with those who are nice to be around, forward thinking, and going somewhere.

If you're in a position to hire employees or choose business associates, you have a golden opportunity to select people with an uplifting attitude. While this requires more effort initially, it can pay big dividends, like enhanced internal morale and fewer people problems, later on. For employees like "gatekeepers," who answer the phone or greet visitors, a pleasant helpful attitude is essential for organizational success. Sour people don't produce great results and negatively affect others.

If the selection process is out of your direct control, be sure to be flexible in forming and maintaining your relationships, and see the good in everyone. This approach works everywhere for everyone, personally and professionally, and it'll reduce your stress and increase your likeability, and everyone will probably be happier.

Associate with other good finders at every opportunity. Find people who are enthusiastic about life and the chance they have each day to make a positive difference, while having fun in the process. Avoid or ignore people who are always moaning and groaning.

Let's say you're a teacher who notices that all your peers seem to do in the teachers' lounge is gossip and complain. Then upon further observation you realize that what's going on isn't confined only to the lounge. It's actually a pervasive losing attitude carried by disgruntled teachers no matter where they go, and it can easily lure the unsuspecting into its deceptive harmful web.

Since you understand that associating with these types of people won't serve you in succeeding, you don't participate. Instead, you read an empowering personal development book someplace where you can concentrate. You remain cordial, but don't spend any more time with those people than you have to as required by your work. If you're tagged as a loner, so be it. It doesn't matter what *they* think. Those people are stress-inducers and success-stealers, and you don't need or want to be around losing influences of any kind.

As you take more charge of your life you choose activities that support your objective of moving forward in making things happen, thereby reducing the negative stress in your life.

Leaders Make Decisions, Then Do Their Best to Make Them Work Out

You may need to make a decision that you don't want to. Sometimes it's simple, but it often involves various elements coupled with anxiety and stress. Therefore, in order to minimize stress, it's important to gather all the facts and make your decision rationally rather than emotionally. Once the decision is made, don't worry about it. Just do your best to make it work out. Then watch the results come in and respond and make adjustments accordingly.

You can weigh the pros and cons of a decision, but if it's ultimately not made or is delayed, anxiety and frustration can result, leading to excessive stress. Therefore, it's to your advantage to become a more effective decision-maker to minimize stress.

Leaders are proactive decision-makers, yet humble enough to ask their mentor for assistance when necessary. Want-to-be leaders who avoid making decisions and don't ask for guidance are less likely to be effective or rise in their organization. Several steps in the decision-making process would include:

- Be sure you know what the situation is. You may need to talk to more than one person to find out.
- Determine the ideal ultimate outcome. What results are you aiming for?
- Gather all the facts and determine possible solutions.
- Look carefully at alternatives and consequences, and weigh them with pro and con lists.
- Make the decision based on your research and consult with your mentor or leader, if necessary.
- Implement the final decision.
- Don't worry. Let your decision have a chance to work out.
- Stay committed to the decision, doing what it takes to make it happen. If for some reason, no matter what you do, it isn't working out, go back to the first step.

I have been able to handle stress over the years by not worrying about my decisions. I simply did my best to make the wisest decision I possibly could, and then relaxed with it.

How Well Do You Use Time and Manage Your Activities?

I also handled stress by working hard, and then playing hard. I traditionally put in long hours, five days a week; however, weekends and vacations were spent in quality time with my family. Since I knew I had put in a productive day, I shut down my thoughts of work as I left the workplace, and looked forward to the next day's challenges and opportunities. I had a winning attitude and had written out my plan for tomorrow before I left for home.

As many do, in addition to your primary job or business, you may have a second job or business. So, for a while, as you're improving your financial picture, you may be managing more activities than usual, which is typical for those accelerating paying down debt, while working to increase their income and raise their standard of living.

So, to keep your stress as low as possible and open up your time outside your main job or business, you may need to get the family together so you can delegate some household chores to other family members. If you don't have children or they aren't old enough to do some of the chores, you may want to hire a neighborhood boy or girl or local handyperson to help you out. For instance, many people could delegate mowing the lawn. This consumes valuable time that could better be used to do something to build your financial future.

Guard your time like the precious commodity it is so you can be productive, not just busy. Once it's gone you can't get it back! Realize how valuable your time really is and invest it wisely so you can keep moving ahead, incrementally achieving your objectives. Then, one, three, five years from now you can look back with a sense of accomplishment...instead of being full of regret.

Reduce Stress by Communicating More Effectively

To minimize stress, both as a leader and in general, it's essential to build strong, mutually beneficial relationships. This requires consistent, effective communication that leads to mutual understanding and appropriate action. Communication isn't just about talking either. It also involves non-verbal elements such as your attitude about the people with whom you're interacting, the way you perceive what's being said, how well you listen, and your eye contact. Then, too, communication also includes your posture, tone of voice, cadence, gestures, and the like.

You communicate best with others on their level of openness in listening to you. If you're sharing your expertise, products, services, or ideas with a prospective customer or associate, their level of openness will be affected by their needs, wants, dreams, or objectives. Listen carefully to their response to your sharing as to how they can benefit from what you have to offer. Can they resolve any of their challenges and get the results they want by buying from or associating with you?

Empathy is a powerful form of non-verbal communication. It's understanding another's feelings and actions, which only comes from a heart-to-heart talk. It allows you to understand where the person is coming from and to vicariously experience their thoughts and actions. You are on their "wavelength," so to speak. This enables you to respond in a manner that allows open authentic communication to flow between the two of you. Because of this accord, you can, therefore, advise and assist more effectively.

Empathy is a winning emotion, sympathy a losing one. Empathy is like throwing a rope to someone down in a hole and encouraging them to pull themselves out, supporting them in their strength to do what it takes to be victorious. But sympathy is when you crawl down in the hole with them and join their "pity party," supporting their weakness. Empathy is an essential quality of a fine leader; a key ingredient to building strong winning relationships.

Another form of non-verbal communication is understanding and using body language. The way you position the various parts of your body, that is, your arms, legs, and eyes, as well as your posture, reflects whether you have an open or closed mind. Folded arms and crossed legs, lack of eye contact, and a rigid posture convey a closed mind and a lack of interest in communicating. When you unfold your arms and uncross your legs, maintain constant eye contact, lean forward, and above all, face the person with whom you are conversing, you communicate open-mindedness.

Listen intently, keep an open mind, and show a keen interest in what is being said. Ask questions to both better understand, as well as to learn all that you can from them. Communicate well nonverbally and it'll support your congruency in verbal communications in a winning way…thereby reducing your stress.

An effective communicator is confident as opposed to aggressive. Aggressive communication comes from emotional reactions that can be abrasive and domineering. Confident communication reflects thoughtful consideration of the situation before talking. As mentioned before, it's best to express your feelings about someone's behavior rather than name-calling, as labeling them can negatively impact their self-esteem, and alienate your relationship.

Aggressive communication actually reinforces the losing behavior, increasing the possibility that it'll occur again! Confident non-arrogant communication is relationship-building rather than relationship-harming. You can still get your point across, but with less likelihood of a defensive negative response.

Your ability to communicate is influenced by your personal and professional history and your perception of a situation. If you're fearful, injured, or in conflict and your emotions are out of control, you may tend to be aggressive. As a result, your communication skills are dulled and ineffective. You won't be able to affect a positive change in the relationship. Instead, you may just start a shouting match which doesn't serve anyone. It will probably inflame both parties and escalate the disagreement into verbal warfare.

Have the self-discipline to cool off first and focus on the behavior. This, along with empathy and forgiveness of yourself and others, can lead to mutually beneficial long-term relationships in all areas. Grow and take your relationships to the next level through thoughtful confident expression of your feelings and ideas.

All Work and No Play...

As the saying goes, *"All work and no play makes Jack a dull boy."* But it may also make him a stressed-out one too.

Stay active to maintain a healthy body and mind. If you don't do anything, you'll soon be bored. When you're most productive at your job or in your business, you're putting your heart in it and enjoying the process as much as you can. After all, it's your life we're talking about here. This is not a dress rehearsal.

As mentioned before, you can blend vacation time in with an out-of-town business trip. Say you're at a convention and you have a free afternoon. Perhaps you can find something fun to do in the area that your whole family would enjoy. You may even meet some new people that day who turn out to be future customers...or even associates! If you can afford it, you could stay an extra couple of days and see the area. Some people have even had business trips abroad and found it a less expensive way to travel with their family.

You could also engage in enjoyable stress-reducing dreambuilding activities along with your other career or business-building activities. Say your company or organization is having a meeting in a hotel in the next town. On the way you could pick up a couple of your associates. You could then drive through a local upscale neighborhood to look at the houses, cruise by a luxury car dealership, and perhaps have a soda or coffee in the hotel's beautiful restaurant. This can be a key ingredient in helping you and your associates fire yourselves up for your dreams.

Since we all need something to go toward to help us maximize our productivity, teach others to take charge and make it happen. Have fun as you go along while building relationships, taking your eyes off yourself which helps you de-stress.

The Importance of Delayed Gratification

Be careful you don't over indulge in recreational activities, especially when you're building your career or business and are in a developmental stage that requires more time and effort. Practicing delayed gratification is key. Perhaps you enjoy and have regularly been participating in a number of sports, coaching, hobbies, or other recreational and volunteer activities.

For example, say you're coaching a soccer team a couple times a week where your son or daughter plays. You may have been doing this type of thing for years. If you have a business-related appointment or event scheduled for that time slot, you may want to have a substitute or assistant coach available to take your role.

Some parents stop sports coaching and many of the other activities they used to participate in so they can free up time to invest in their business or profession. To compensate, they diligently blend as much fun as they can with their normal business activities, thereby to reducing stress, while staying on track with their goals.

Decide for yourself what's best in the long run for you and your family. When you invest time now in building your career or business, say to reach certain financial goals, you may be doing it to reap the time later so you can have more time with your family. Or you can golf, fish, bike, hike, boat, fly, hunt, ski, bowl, or participate in whatever activities appeal to you even more because you've reached your goals. It's truly a balancing act; freeing up the time, working it out to have as much joy as possible, while devoting the necessary time to pursue your dreams and goals.

Adopt the Attitude of "I Enjoy Life!"

Enjoying your everyday tasks, in concert with the building of your business or career, helps you to be lighthearted. This approach also helps you to reduce the stress, anxiety, and frustrations that are harmful to your overall health.

Again, take yourself lightly, but what you're doing seriously. Laugh a lot and poke fun at yourself, but not at others. Laughter, as discussed before, which often results from a good-natured attitude, is also a powerful "medicine" for managing stress; and it's free! Be cheerful, uplifting others anywhere you happen to be, and notice the difference in how *you* feel. When you exude high energy you're more likely to attract winning-thinking people into your life. So do your best to interject some levity into your life every day, especially when you're having a challenging day. It'll help you have a stress-free attitude.

How Happy Are You with Your Job?

A lot of people are stressed-out because they haven't thoughtfully chosen their job, or perhaps something has changed in the meantime. They may have taken the first decent-paying job they were offered, even though the work didn't interest them very much or maybe not at all! Or perhaps their parents expected them to work in a particular field or in the family business. And much to their chagrin, just to please them, they went in that direction.

A lack of purposeful self-direction gets people in trouble. They do things for the wrong reasons, rather than what's in their heart. They fail to follow their dream and, as a result, lead less happy and not as meaningful lives as they could. They often feel stuck, but it's only their thinking that makes it seem like they have no choice.

Do you feel stuck? If so, you're not alone. It was *you* who chose what you do for a living. Sure, you may have let someone influence you in the process but, nonetheless, it was and still is your choice; and you can choose to change that at any time. It's up to you.

Are you watching the clock all day, wishing for the week to fly by so you can enjoy the weekend, or are you doing something toward creating a richer, more rewarding life? Do you enjoy your work, or just believe it's your lot in life to endure until you can retire many years from now? Do you have children you want or feel you have to put through college? Is there some reason you've been using to justify not doing something to improve your life situation, financially and otherwise, perhaps on the side?

If you're unhappy with your job you're negatively affecting not only yourself, but others as well! So...what could you possibly do to make things better? Many people want things to change, but excuse themselves from taking action saying, "That's easier said than done." While that's certainly true, the more worthwhile something is the more effort it requires to accomplish. While it's normal to want things easy, we can't learn from easy. Easy isn't the way to a happier, more successful, meaningful life either!

Are You Really Being Honest with Yourself?

Are you tempted to just stay in your comfort zone, which is probably more like a "familiar zone"... because it's really not all that comfortable anymore? Have you been rationalizing for a while that your situation really isn't all that bad?

But think about it. Isn't rationalizing just telling yourself rational-sounding lies? For example, let's say you basically enjoy your job, but your boss seems to be taking you for granted. To add insult to injury, you may be making less money and working longer hours than you'd like. What rationalization might such a busy underpaid, under-appreciated employee say to avoid making a change to a new job or building a business on the side? They might say something like…"I'm too busy"; "I don't know anything else"; "It pays the bills"; or "Good jobs are hard to find."

Do you like your job or have you outgrown it? Are you ready for a bigger challenge and more responsibility? Have you talked to your mentor or boss about it? Are you less productive because you really don't care anymore? Do you need to change careers and do something more suitable to your objectives?

Are you going to follow your heart, your dream, and do what you know you really, really want and sincerely need to do for your own sanity, if nothing else? Or are you just venting your frustrations, resigned to surviving day by day? Do you realize that maintaining the status quo isn't even possible? If you're trying to do so you're actually losing ground, as time, the most precious commodity you have, is going away. Are you setting yourself up for regret by not working toward living the life that's in your heart to live?

Did those questions help you get a grip on where you are and where you want to go? What new insights have you gained? Write them down. Then look back over the questions, as you may be struck with yet another question that you would do well to answer. Or perhaps you'll gain another helpful insight. For example, have you been procrastinating in taking action concerning your income situation? If so, ask yourself, "What do I need to be doing next that I've been putting off?" and "When am I going to do it?" This could be something as important as talking with your boss, leader, or mentor to discuss your situation and explore the possibilities. How about it?

Change Your Work, Change Your Attitude…or Change Both!

I remember a neighbor friend who, like many, hated almost every hour he spent at work. He could hardly wait until retirement, even though it was years away. How stressed he must have felt every day. I suggested that he change jobs and/or find a business he could do on the side that would give him hope for a brighter future and to live a more meaningful life. But as most do he kept complaining, not taking any action to improve his situation.

Many people are unhappy and stressed out with their work, in a rut so deeply that it's almost like a grave with the ends kicked out! They don't seem to realize that what they're thinking and doing, day in day out, is only perpetuating a seemingly endless struggle. Then, of course, there are average-thinking people who wouldn't be happy even if a million dollars fell into their laps. Sure as the earth is round, they'd still find something to complain about!

For them, an overall change of attitude is essential before they can unlock the door to a new life. They can begin simply by looking inside themselves for the root cause of their unhappiness and stress to gain a new perspective, change their attitude, and then take the actions necessary to make the desired change.

Next, they could help themselves tremendously by becoming "good finders" who look for and appreciate the positives they already have in their work, as well in other areas of life. Then they can make any changes with their new "attitude of gratitude," and attract other such people to team up with.

I once met a 77-year-old who had been unhappy and stressed out most of his life. But I'm happy to report that he changed his life. How did he do it? When he was 70 someone introduced him to personal growth through self-help books. He started reading and creating a better life for himself. He admitted, "I was obnoxious for 70 of my 76 years...until I read that first book. I sometimes slip back into my old ways, but it doesn't last very long! I'm still working on it." He changed his attitude about everything, especially people. He learned to care about and respect them ... to love them ... instead of being self-centered, obstinate, and combative.

He also learned how to turn around what appears to be a losing situation and find the benefit(s) in it. He learned to forgive and actually went to people toward whom he had harbored negative feelings, totally forgiving them...and himself. I was pleased to hear he had even learned to take better care of his health. He proved that it's never too late to change your attitude...and change your life.

Those who grumble about everything, regardless of how good their life and work may actually be, would do well to end their losing thinking. They could start simply by making a list of all the positive things about what they do and have.

One way some people reduce stress is by making a job or career change. But one of the greatest ways is when they take more charge of their life by building an independent business from home on the side. This can be done flexibly by blending it in with their personal and work schedules, taking one step at a time as they get moving, gaining momentum, doing whatever it takes.

Many people, however, simply need to get serious about expanding the business or profession they're already in. If they're griping that it's not growing, it's probably because they're just maintaining what they have instead of building on it. They could benefit from the product and leadership training available in their industry.

A goal like advancing to new levels cannot be accomplished at the same level of knowledge, experience, and understanding on which the goal was set. Those who want to move ahead will benefit from learning to first better lead themselves, before they can become a role model who can then more effectively lead others.

In the job world, people can easily be *forced* to make a change by being laid off through no fault of their own, or fired for whatever reason. Their employer may close down, be merged, or bought out, making employees quite vulnerable. It's far better to be the one initiating the change, rather than being the surprised, unprepared recipient of a forced change. Makes sense, doesn't it?

It's far less stressful to take charge now, proactively working toward preparing yourself for whatever could potentially challenge your income situation. This will bolster your hope and increase your peace of mind, and can also be downright exciting!

One way to gain more control over your life could be taking full advantage of the business or profession you're already in. Take action, and keep going and growing, learning all you can as to how you can make it happen. Who knows where it could all lead? It's definitely worth doing, regardless of whether or not you believe you're vulnerable to losing your job or getting a cut in pay. After all, things change!

Another option, of course, is simply to accept your lot in life… and continue being frustrated, unhappy, and stressed out to whatever degree. But doing nothing to better your situation is a losing proposition that keeps you stuck, going nowhere. Don't depend on anything getting better all by itself. You've got to take charge and make it happen! You'll be glad you did.

How Stress Almost Killed Me!

I loved my career; and even though there was stress involved, I managed it with a winning can-do attitude. The only pressure to produce was self-imposed, which I handled well for years… using a blend of Type A and Type B characteristics. However, three years before my planned retirement a dangerously stressful situation developed that I failed to manage very well.

It all began after I decided to retire early, not mentioning my plans to the corporation, my associates, peers, friends, or even my mentor. Unfortunately, my unwillingness to share this life-changing decision with anyone outside my family caused me to become more and more stressed by my daily activities.

I had prevented myself from receiving the additional support and guidance I could have experienced had I been more open. Many make the mistake of not sharing their concerns, especially major ones, with those who could have been supportive. Mistakenly thinking they can handle it all on their own can be a truly life-threatening decision, as mine turned out to be!

I got so wrapped up in winding down and putting things in order that I failed to see the signs of stress I had previously recognized and managed so well. Then when things weren't going as planned I started becoming irritable and ever more uncomfortable that I still hadn't shared my plans with anyone outside the family. No one in my agency knew what was coming.

I finally broke the news in late November with my last day in the office to be in mid-December. I felt grateful for having had the opportunity to grow personally and professionally, fulfilling my potential and making family dreams come true. Building a successful business by helping people also contributed to giving my life greater meaning. However, I was ready to enjoy more of what my loving wife and I wanted to do, while giving back in a bigger way.

Even so, I found it quite stressful having put myself in the position of suddenly needing to announce my retirement and then saying a quick goodbye to people I considered friends who I had mentored and cared about over the years. I had boxed myself in, inconsiderate of others' feelings and their need to transition leadership and training, shocking everyone, even my mentor.

The Big Attack

Incredibly, I soon suffered a near-fatal heart attack! Once the initial trauma had passed and I calmed down, I asked the doctor, "Why?" Unfortunately, he couldn't give me a satisfactory answer, not even mentioning that stress could have been a factor, even though the medical community was starting to see a connection.

But as touched on earlier, it has since been recognized that aggression (hostility), coupled with not showing any positive emotion, like joy and appreciation, are factors that could lead to high blood pressure and coronary artery disease… the cause of most heart attacks. Thankfully, being achievement-oriented is not the problem!

Really wanting to retire, I had let my secretly held plans and frustrations grow into, and I'm ashamed to admit, thoughtlessness of others, which evolved into aggressive (hostile) behavior, which almost killed me! While I had managed stress well for over 35 years, during my last year of work I felt I had paid my dues and was ready to move on. I didn't want anything to get in the way of my plan or anyone to try to talk me out of it.

Preoccupied, I had ignored several signs of stress that had I been more aware would have noticed and done something about. For example, in retrospect, there were times during my last year when I became impatient, even aggressive, with a customer or associate I felt was behaving unreasonably. I remember tensing up, becoming short of breath, my heart rate accelerating. But since the tension had melted away shortly after the encounters were over, I never gave them a second thought.

In addition to those experiences, right before the attack I remember becoming short of breath on two particular occasions. Once, while briskly walking on the cart path of our golf course, I suddenly had difficulty breathing. I didn't think anything of it since as soon as I stopped and rested for a few seconds, the feeling left. Two days later the same thing happened; this time while I was swimming. Regrettably, I ignored these signs since I thought I was in good health, had excellent stamina, and felt energetic.

Could YOU Be Ignoring the Signs of Stress?

Unfortunately, people all too often overlook the warning signs ...whatever they may be...of serious illness. My body was telling me something, but I wasn't paying attention. Is your body trying to tell you something?

Whenever your body talks to you ... listen! This could enable you to avoid a challenge, catching it before it becomes serious or could even lead to sudden death. If you're experiencing a symptom or symptoms that could be warning you of a health challenge, be sure to consult with your physician, ask questions, and perhaps get a second opinion. Do it for yourself and those who love and care about you.

To further emphasize the need for alertness regarding your own body talk and the need to question your physician, I'll share an experience where even my family doctor ignored a warning sign! I had my annual physical exam two months before my retirement. My blood pressure was elevated to 160 over 90, while my history showed that it had always been 120 over 60. My doctor advised me to have it checked every day at the same time for ten days. I did this, and it slowly went back to its normal level. But it, too, turned out to be a false indicator that I was okay...but I wasn't!

I believe stress caused the increase in my previously consistent healthy blood pressure, which would have alerted my physician. I rationalized ignoring it because I had a lot on my mind and was very busy, so I didn't take seriously what my body was telling me. But since health is a personal responsibility, I should have taken steps to determine the cause. By failing to see my doctor, I suffered the consequences ... as we all do when we don't take appropriate action. Chances are proper diagnosis and treatment would have reduced the severity of my heart attack, or perhaps prevented it altogether.

Fortunately, I was one of those who survived their first heart attack; and I'm grateful I was given a second chance at life and an opportunity to share some valuable information with you. Hopefully, you won't have to go through the same type of undiagnosed (or diagnosed, for that matter) stress-related illness. Take whatever preventative wellness measures it takes to avoid it.

Living Healthier

Since the heart attack, I've taken the recommended steps to live with a damaged heart, and feel as good as or better than I've ever felt. I avoid stressful situations, don't take myself too seriously, take challenging situations in stride, truly care about people, and don't concern myself with the things I can't control. I've also improved my health habits—maintaining a diet of low fat, low cholesterol foods, taking vitamins and supplements, coupled with regular exercise, which helped me recover both mentally and physically.

Since stress can be as silent a killer as hypertension, it's best to get with your doctor to develop a plan to manage and control it so you can minimize and ideally eliminate its potentially devastating effects. To get winning results begin with a winning attitude. According to the Mayo Clinic...

> *"When your state of mind is generally optimistic, you're better able to handle everyday stress in a more constructive way. That ability may contribute to the widely observed health benefits of positive thinking."*

Continually Learning for Greater Success

Top-performing organizations, corporations, and leaders know the value of continuing education, which could consist of: books, audios, videos, product fairs and demos, training sessions, seminars, conventions, webinars, and other resources and events that can increase their people's knowledge, enthusiasm, and productivity. I'm convinced that this is vital not only for greater success and happiness professionally as well as personally, but also for your physical, mental, and emotional well-being. Perhaps that's why you're reading this book.

People all over the world, including those who've been at the "bottom," financially or otherwise, have enriched their lives in so many ways by taking advantage of the learning materials and opportunities made available by their employers, leaders, or mentors. I know first-hand how vital this is for success, not only from building my agency, but also in creating a great personal and family life. Our development as fulfilled, contributing members of society is directly related to our committed participation in learning and real-life application of the time-tested principles, people skills, and specialized knowledge essential for success, personally and professionally.

Blending Type A and B for Health, Leadership, and Success

Since you're concerned about the quality of your life now and in the future, earnestly commit to creating the life you've dreamed of. To maximize your potential in doing so, you'll want to incorporate the best of the Type A and B behavior characteristics. Growing into them day by day, it's likely you'll be transitioning from qualities that may be either too laid back or pressure inducing, to more of a self-assured (not arrogant), forward moving (not aggressive), confidence-inducing, sincerely caring-about-others approach.

To get what you want in life may require a change personally or professionally, or both. You'll be working toward gaining more control over your life, which bolsters your attitude and reduces stress. You're probably already aware of the benefits of a healthy lifestyle and desire to live the best life you can.

So continue or upgrade the health habits of regular exercise, eating more healthfully, maintaining a healthy weight and appearance, and taking vitamins, minerals, and supplements, which are also key ingredients to living a healthier, more successful life. We'll cover more on this later. As always, consult with your family doctor and ask what he or she recommends.

Now's the time to move on from the stress of not living the life you want, and start crossing the bridge to the life you've always dreamed of. Be harmonious with your deepest desires and become the person you were created to be.

"Lack of activity destroys the good condition of every human being, while movement and methodical physical exercise preserve it."

—Plato

"One should eat to live, not live to eat."

—Benjamin Franklin

—3—

Do Your Health Habits Support Greater Success?

"Those who think they have no time for exercise will sooner or later have to find time for illness." —Dr. Edward Stanley

A WINNING ATTITUDE, COUPLED WITH regular exercise and a healthy diet is essential for being more productive...so you can create greater success, happiness, and meaning in life. And since your mind and body affect each other as an integrated whole, both are equally important. Use your winning attitude to empower yourself to be healthier, knowing a sound body supports a sound mind.

A winning attitude leads to taking winning actions, which builds self-esteem. Together with a healthy diet and regular exercise, this all helps to improve the state of your mind and body, and their functions, thereby improving the quality of your life ... a priceless gift that only you can give to yourself!

Many people wonder why they don't feel so great much of the time, having developed losing habits that make it difficult for them to get and stay fit. They don't exercise regularly, except in moving food from the container or their plate to their mouths, and walking to and from their vehicle. They consume rich, sugary, high-calorie, high cholesterol, fat-producing foods and drinks, and often eat too much too fast with little, if any, attention to a balanced diet. With a catch-as-catch-can attitude, they just stuff food in their face on the run.

For best results, combine regular exercise with a heart-healthy diet low in saturated fats, cholesterol, sugar, and sodium, and high in fiber. Also, the American Heart Association says to keep hydrated to better enable the heart to pump blood to the muscles, helping them work efficiently, and recommends getting enough sleep as well.

Keep in mind now that heart disease is the number one killer in the world! So for maximum health, success, and happiness pay careful attention to what you're doing health-wise to keep this vital organ in good working order. The quality of your life, especially as you get older, depends on it.

Dieting without exercise causes the loss of muscle and water weight as well as some fat loss. However, consistent exercise will help burn fat and keep you from regaining the weight you've lost by adopting healthy eating habits. The key is good habits...the missing piece for many yo-yo dieters. They never got into the habit of consistently exercising and eating a balanced diet of nutritious food in the right quantities to maintain their new slimmer self. Healthy eating, along with taking appropriate supplements, getting enough sleep, and participating in a good exercise program is the most effective way for most people to control their weight while helping their heart.

According to the US Department of Health and Human Services (HHS), regular physical activity helps prevent risk factors such as high blood pressure and weight gain, and protects against chronic illnesses like heart disease, stroke, some cancers, Type 2 diabetes, and depression. It's associated with improved quality of life, emotional well-being, positive mental health, and healthy aging ... and may delay the onset of cognitive decline in older adults.

HHS recommends that adults get at least 150 minutes of moderate-intensity aerobic physical activity or 75 minutes of vigorous-intensity physical activity, or an equivalent combination, each week. Those who are inactive or don't yet meet the guidelines are strongly encouraged to work toward this goal.

But whatever you do, be sure to check with your physician before making any changes to your diet or exercise habits. They can make specific recommendations in line with your particular needs. While these ideas and activities have worked well for many, suggestions shared here aren't to be considered personal medical guidance.

But I'm Too Busy...I Don't Have the Time!

"When am I going to find the time for regular exercise?" you may ask. Never! You'll *never* just find it. Instead, you need to *take* the time and invest it in your health and well-being. After all, you have the same 24 hours-a-day that everyone else has. As challenging as it may be we all take the time to do the things we really want to or need to do, don't we? No one makes excuses for that!

In the past you may have taken time for a long lunch, squandered your precious time watching negative news and success-stealing TV shows and movies, or did other nonproductive tasks that can't contribute to the future you say you'd love to have. So why not *start taking time now* for something that can help you move in the direction of your dreams, goals, and objectives?

Making exercise a priority is the first step, even if you don't like doing it. That's okay. You want to live a better life, right? The healthier you are the more you can enjoy life. Committing to a program and devoting time to it is the next step. Exercise is an investment in you toward feeling your best, being successful and happier, and finding more meaning and fulfillment in all you do,

Buy some good walking shoes or sneakers ... and use them! Set your alarm a-half-hour-or-so earlier in the morning. It's a beautiful and refreshing time for exercising and taking a brisk walk, releasing those endorphins. And while you're becoming healthier and invigorated, be sure to listen to an educational or motivational audio.

There may be times when you think you're too tired to exercise. However, once you get moving it'll help relieve your fatigue and stress. Once you start a program you'll feel better physically, and +also give yourself a more alert mind which will help you be more productive and better able to handle any challenges that arise.

Establish the exercise habit...a winning one that will be part of your routine for the rest of your life. Commit to following your program and reap the benefits, experiencing a tremendous feeling of self-mastery, joy, and freedom. Winners exert self-control and do the right thing, whether they feel like it or not!

What could be more personally gratifying than building a sound body, enhancing your well-being while strengthening your heart? Remember that you could have all the success in the world, but without good health you won't enjoy it nearly as much, or perhaps not at all...depending on your condition.

A few more winning benefits of regular exercise include:

- It helps lower high blood pressure.
- It increases HDL (good cholesterol).
- It burns fat and helps you maintain a healthy weight.
- Your resting heart rate will decrease, enabling it to work more efficiently.

- Your appetite is decreased due to a higher metabolism.
- It improves your body shape by strengthening muscles and reducing fat.
- It helps relieve anger, depression, and anxiety.
- You'll be in higher spirits and better able to take charge and make it happen.
- It reduces your stress level, a major factor in causing illness.
- You'll sleep better.

Mentally and Physically Fit People Handle Stress Better

There are people who have a natural ability to handle stress. Just as there are differences in other traits...such as hair and skin colors, height and weight, build and intelligence...there's also a difference in everyone's ability to tolerate and manage stress. Anyone who's mentally and physically fit is stronger, and therefore, can withstand stress far better than those who aren't. As Dr. Malcolm Carruthers warned...

> *"The combination of high emotional activity, together with low physical activity deranges body chemistry and is the major cause of heart disease."*

Know anyone in that situation?

What's an Effective Aerobic Exercise Program?

The key ingredient is to have continuous activity that increases your heart rate to a safe level for 20 to 40 minutes. Exercises that don't maintain the increase in your heart rate—those that give you short periods of high activity followed by periods of low activity, such as weightlifting, golf, tennis, baseball, football, and bowling—aren't substitutes for sustained aerobic exercise.

Aerobic exercise can be brisk walking, running, jogging, rowing, cycling, and swimming. I find that a 40-minute brisk walk at a pace of a 13-minute mile or 135 paces per minute increases my heart rate to my target level. Your target level is the maximum you need to achieve and sustain during exercise, and it depends on your resting rate. Be sure to establish this with your doctor's supervision.

Whenever the weather is too cold, windy, hot, or humid, I ride a stationary bike or walk a treadmill for the same period of time at the same pace. While doing so, it's great to also listen to a success audio or read a personal development book! However, as some people do, if you choose to walk outdoors regardless of the weather, it's always beneficial to listen to something positive.

Exercise can improve the function of your heart and the efficiency of your cardiovascular system. Even so, a minimum of a five-minute warm-up period prior to exercise and a ten-minute cool down afterward are essential.

A warm-up allows your heart and cardiovascular system time to adjust and supply the blood and oxygen required by your body during exercise. If your heart and surrounding blood vessels and arteries are damaged this warm-up is even more important to accommodate the extra demands of exercise.

Light calisthenics and stretching loosens your muscles, and helps prevent the damage that could result if you would pick up your pace too quickly. Start slowly and gradually increase your pace. The slow progression helps to protect your heart and circulatory system as it works harder to meet the increasing demands you're placing on it.

Cooling down allows your body to slow down gradually following the exercise. Stretching reduces muscle tightness induced by exertion and gives your cardiovascular system a chance to readjust. Let any perspiration evaporate rather than toweling it off, since it provides natural cooling. Delay taking a hot shower or eating solid foods for at least 30 minutes, and drink plenty of fluids, preferably water, to replenish those lost.

My Good Physical Condition Saved My Life

I began exercising decades ago, but didn't gear my program toward helping my heart to be as healthy as I do today. Like a lot of people do, I started because I wanted to lose weight. Then later, I read that exercise is good for both body and mind.

When I had a heart attack 30 years ago, my doctors told me that being in good physical condition was a major reason why I survived. My illness was caused by the blockage of the left descending coronary artery that had apparently been gradually closing for some time. Amazingly, however, when an EKG (electrocardiogram) was taken six months before, it was totally normal.

The point is, if I hadn't been exercising all those years, even though it was limited in scope, I may have died as a result of that attack. I now do cardiovascular exercises as I described earlier. This program was recommended by my cardiologist, and it consisted of three one-hour sessions each week at a cardiac rehabilitation center where I slowly worked into the program I now use on my own. Your physician can recommend an exercise program to suit your own needs. It can be simple to do, yet crucial to your overall well-being and perhaps, like me, even your very survival!

Many hospitals have a cardiac rehab program for patients with a history of heart disease, diabetes, high blood pressure, and high cholesterol levels. After completing six months of such a monitored program, I continue to follow their recommendations for maximum effectiveness. I check my pulse rate before, during, and after exercise to be sure I don't exceed my target rate. Your physician can teach you how to check your pulse rate.

Take advantage of free opportunities to check your blood pressure and pulse, perhaps at a pharmacy or other location. Take it once, then take it a second time after taking four deep breaths in through your nose, hold four seconds, and exhale slowly through your mouth. Notice how your blood pressure and pulse lower after doing this calming breathing exercise. You might be surprised.

Most people can improve their chances for a happy, positive, healthy life simply by making a few important changes in their habits. Two of the most foundational changes you can make are in your diet and exercise habits, so be sure to schedule time for a systematic program. Thirty minutes a day, along with improved eating habits, could make quite a positive difference in your health and life overall. In addition to your enhanced well-being, your increased and more effective productivity, alone, could more than make up for the time and energy you invest in making these changes.

Many business owners and other leaders realize the importance of physical fitness to productivity, and some have even established programs for their executives and regular employees. If that's the case where you work, join in on the fun and help your body and mind stay fit and strong. It could pay you big dividends! You could probably even fit it in over your lunch period. If not, as mentioned before, maybe you could simply take a brisk walk during lunch or at break-time(s). You'll soon have developed a new, fun, and rewarding habit—one that you'll be doing almost automatically, without conscious thought. Then it becomes easier to do, and you'll feel deprived if you miss it.

As you continue healthy eating and exercise habits your general outlook will improve and you'll be more self-motivated. Excellent health gives you the winning energy, vitality, and stamina to do whatever it takes to move forward in life.

How Committed Are You?

"No one can know the potential of a
life committed to win;
With courage it faces the challenge to
achieve great success in the end!

"So explore the dimensions of greatness,
And believe that the world can be won;
By a mind that is fully committed,
Knowing the task can be done!

"Your world has no place for the skeptic,
No room for the doubter to stand;
To weaken your firm resolution,
That you can excel in this land!

"We must have vision to see our potential,
And faith to believe what we see;
Then courage to act with conviction,
To become what God meant us to be!

"So possess the strength and the courage,
To conquer whatever you choose;
It's the person who never gets started,
Who's destined forever to lose!"

—Author Unknown

—4—

How Motivated Are You for Greater Success?

"Flaming enthusiasm, backed up by common sense and persistence, is the quality that most frequently makes for success."
—Dale Carnegie

WHAT MOTIVATES YOU? "Motivation" is defined as—"to provide with a motive." Whereas "motive" is defined as—"something, such as a need, desire, dream, goal, or objective that causes a person to act; *moving* to action."

The need for money motivates most people to work a job...so they can pay the bills! But they're also motivated by many intangibles like: peace of mind, appreciation, recognition, happiness, joy, love, friendship, a great marriage and family, and more control over their life, coupled with getting ahead, and a more meaningful life. While you can be encouraged by others and inspired by their accomplishments, no one else can motivate you! It's something you have to do for yourself; it comes from within.

Winners have the habit of self-motivation. They energetically talk to themselves with a winning attitude, silently as well as aloud, motivating themselves to take action. They literally *activate* themselves into doing something greater than what they've already done. It's incredibly powerful to emotionally proclaim your intention and what you expect to accomplish. Encouraging yourself mentally and verbally is essential in helping you do what you need to do!

Winners also use "tools" to motivate themselves. Hungry for their dreams to come true, they take advantage of the personal and professional growth tools that their leaders or mentors recommend. How about you? How motivated are you for greater success?

Several winning ingredients are key factors in helping you gain and maintain your motivation to take action. The most essential of these are desire, faith, belief, caring about others, enthusiasm, commitment, and persistence. While desire is at the top of the list, you also need the other ingredients coupled with consistent appropriate action…in order to be more productive, get ahead, and live the happier more fulfilling life you want.

Desire is more than wishing or hoping for something to happen. Someone who just wishes and hopes for what they want, rather than taking action to obtain it, is undoubtedly a person who just watches things happen. Most people, unfortunately, fall into this category.

The person who makes things happen has a strong, unrelenting, burning desire coupled with belief and determination. They have faith, enthusiasm, and a love of people as they persistently blast through the obstacles and take ownership of the theme of this book —take charge and make it happen. Since it's your dream, it's your responsibility to make it your reality.

How Much Do You Want Your Dream or Objective?

Without desire, not much, if anything, happens. Once you have established a desire for your dream in your mind and heart, follow through with a definite plan of action to reach your goal. Desire alone won't make it miraculously appear. That's just wishful thinking. The action and sacrifice necessary in accomplishing your goal is a price you need to pay.

Are you willing to pay the price? If so, perhaps your mentor or leader can help you develop an action plan. Successful people have vision. They mentally picture what they really want to accomplish—their dream or objective. This helps them generate a burning desire that serves as the trigger that fires them up and sets them into motion toward the fruition of their desire.

Fortify Your Belief in Yourself and Your Company

A strong belief in yourself and what you're doing is necessary to stir the passion to make your dream an obsession. Open your mind and super-charge yourself with an unassailable belief in your dream by focusing on it and getting impassioned with it. Step outside the box of your old way of thinking and you'll realize that there is no limit to what you can do … as long as you believe strongly enough. A closed mind with preconceived thoughts and limits will not nurture a strong belief; it will only hold you back.

Continue opening your mind to upgrade your thinking as to the vast potential within you, while embracing the possibilities before you. As you increase your knowledge and motivation, your belief in yourself and the fine company you've chosen to associate with will strengthen, and your zeal to make real the dream that's dear to your heart will grow. When you build your business or career to new levels, your self-esteem and confidence will fortify, further bolstering your belief. In the process, be sure to associate with those who are where you want to be, and support others in doing so as well.

As you grow and move forward, you'll continue attracting more self-motivated, success-oriented people, leading the way by your powerful winning example. It's a fun, challenging process. True leaders, and those aspiring to be so, are always upgrading their knowledge and skills to serve more effectively. How about you? What are you doing to be a leader in your field?

When you have strong belief and a burning desire for achievement, you can accomplish anything you sincerely set your mind and heart to. Any fear of failure and feeling that your goals are impossible to achieve will be history. You focus on what *can* be done, rather than what you may have thought couldn't be done. If things don't go as planned you remain confident in yourself, your company and organization, certain you can still reach your goal. Your winning achievement-oriented mentality can pay big dividends.

Make Persistence Your Middle Name

Persistence is another key factor in staying motivated. When it's blended with belief, desire, and action, your dream can become reality. Without persistence not much is accomplished. Go forward with resolution doing what you know is right for you in spite of any opposition or warning from others who aren't where you want to be and may just be envious of your ambition.

Don't let anything get in the way of you accomplishing your objective. Do everything necessary to resolve any situation that threatens to thwart your efforts. Stay focused on your previously decided-upon direction. Doggedness and perseverance to stay the course and to do whatever it takes describes persistent winners. They reset their goals, as necessary, until they reach their objective.

How Action-Oriented Are You?

Are you the kind of person who regularly talks about doing great things yet fails to follow through? Do you walk your talk? Are you a pacesetter? Have you taken charge and started taking action toward your dream?

No matter what detrimental habits you may have developed to date, you can replace them with beneficial ones and become more successful…starting right now. It's as simple as taking one tiny step in the direction of your dream, which could be just writing it down.

If you haven't written your dream down on paper, or in your phone, dare to go ahead and do it right now. You could begin simply with "My dream is…."

A burning desire, coupled with belief, persistence, and appropriate consistent action will, when strongly and positively directed, result in the personal motivation required to carry you onward to the realization of your dream.

How Positive and Excited Are You?

Many years ago, I attended my first motivational seminar. It was valuable because it reinforced the success principles I had learned and applied throughout my career. It encouraged winning thinking and going in the direction of my dream, and spurred me on with an encouraging "I-did-it-and-you-can-do-it-too" message. The seminar leader's goal was to help us have a happier, more exciting, fulfilling, prosperous, meaningful, and overall better life.

The leader used an exciting tone of voice and words such as… wonderful, terrific, fired-up, outstanding, great, fantastic, super, and excellent. Using such power-packed winning words and an upbeat tone of voice as a part of your everyday language can have an enormous impact on the quality of your life.

How do most people respond to, "How are you today"? They generally give you a low-energy blah-tone response of "Not bad," "So, so," or "Okay." Whenever the weather isn't sunny and clear, you're likely to hear "What a lousy day!" In the summer here in the US, many people complain that it's too hot, while in the winter they say it's too cold. When it's raining they say it's dreary.

Those phrases focus on the negative rather than the positive aspects of the weather. But how about focusing on the positive to uplift yourself and others? For example, if it's raining you could say, "We really need the rain," if that's true. Or you could call it "liquid sunshine." Or you could decide not to comment on the weather at all and, instead, focus your attention on the person you're talking to. You could sincerely compliment them for something positive you notice about them, and listen to what they have to say.

Choose to make a positive difference. If you say and do what the average-thinking person says and does, you'll get average results. Average results aren't what you want...or you wouldn't be reading this book, now would you?

So in response to the question "How are you today?" you could say..."Happy to see you!" or "I'm doing well; thanks for asking!" You'll upgrade and enrich your life by displaying a winning attitude and you may be surprised by the pleasant reactions of others.

I vividly recall such an experience while on a business trip, having breakfast at the restaurant of a major motel chain. The hostess greeted me with the typical, "How are you this morning?" My enthusiastic response, "Wonderful!" brought a smile to her face as she quipped, "Gee, can it really be that good this early in the morning?" I chortled, "You bet it can! It all depends on your attitude."

My publisher often answers... "I'm thankful!" If someone asks him, "Why?" he sincerely honors them, affirming... "For you and what you do!" He turns what would ordinarily be bland exchanges into extraordinary, even if brief, experiences that can boost someone else's spirits, and well as his own! You can do the same.

By using an uplifting tone of voice and winning words and phrases in your responses, in most cases you'll experience cheerful reactions. Brighten other people's day with your optimistic, sunny disposition. Be a people magnet. You may well be nurturing a relationship with someone you'll be associating with in some important way in the future. But regardless of whether you'll ever talk to someone again, be an encourager every day.

Consider this. If you agree with the statement "Isn't it a lousy day?" you're not helping the person who thinks this way. Their losing attitude will only create losing results. They'll get what they expect—the worst! You'd also be reinforcing their losing thoughts in your own mind, which will hurt rather than help you.

Speak only winning words. You may feel uncomfortable and awkward the first few times. But after 21 days, speaking with a winning focus will become a habit—a wonderful, happy, success-inducing habit. You'll be a pleasure to be around and more likely to attract other winning-thinking people to you, which is great for building your business or career.

Maintain Winning Thoughts...No Matter What!

Even though winning thoughts are prerequisite for success, vast numbers of people still don't embrace that, as they continue dwelling on losing thoughts. They believe their situation is caused by factors beyond their control…that they can't do anything about it.

Refusing to take personal responsibility for the part they played in contributing to the situation they're in, they blame something or someone else, doing no more than complaining about it. So their losing thinking keeps them stuck. No matter what their circumstances may be, thinking winning thoughts is the only choice that can lead to victory over the situation.

Our environment is inundated with negativity and other people's agendas that many allow to distract them from achieving their objectives, preventing them from living their purpose and reaching their potential. So some contend it's impossible to have a winning attitude. But that's only an excuse. Don't believe it! There are countless people of all ethnic backgrounds, income and educational levels, races, and religions…with numerous challenges, big and small. However, they do whatever it takes to maintain a winning mental attitude which, like most things in life, is simply a choice.

There are leaders throughout the world, especially those who seemingly had little or nothing going for them, who took charge, ascended the ranks, and made a bigger difference. While caring about others they developed a mental toughness, fighting with all their might to rise above the negativity of their environment, causing them to grow through the challenges they encountered. They are among the truly successful, leading happier, more rewarding and meaningful lives.

Such leaders are an inspiration and fine role models to many others who previously thought they were locked into a depressingly negative environment. They may appear to be lucky, but they've overcome many obstacles to get to where they are.

Now here's something else to think about. All progress would stop if the world was run by those who said it couldn't be done or pegged it all on luck. It works the same way in your life too.

At one time, most people would have thought electricity was impossible. While that may be hard to believe, the same thing was thought of the telephone, railroads, automobiles, airplanes, orbiting the earth, going to the moon, the Internet, and endless other innovations and accomplishments that we now benefit from. What if the people behind those developments would have had a losing can't-do attitude? What if they had taken the losing "advice" of those who called them crazy, while putting them and their endeavors down? Where would we all be today?

Monitor and control your thoughts about your goals and dreams, and develop and maintain a winning attitude about yourself, your abilities, and what you're doing. Belief in yourself and a winning can-do attitude are two of the most important attributes you can have as you work toward your objectives, especially if they seem unrealistic. Like the great innovators experienced, people who put you down may call *you* crazy when *you* start something new or are pursuing a dream. Then after you succeed they simply say you're lucky, a typical response of average-thinking people who may simply be jealous.

Do you want to rise to leadership (or higher leadership) in your organization? Do you want to make a winning difference in the lives of others? Have you noticed that the finest leaders are kind, considerate people? They have a winning attitude, care about others, and do their best to help them succeed or benefit in some way. They subscribe to the idea that you can achieve what you desire in life provided you help enough other people achieve what they desire.

Successful people think success and through enough consistent appropriate action, they achieve it. Sure they fail along the way, but they learn and keep going. They expect the best of themselves and encourage others to do their best as well. They don't make excuses but rather take full responsibility for their life and their results, and they encourage others to do the same. They refuse to play the "blame game," knowing it leads nowhere.

True achievers understand that "success" is defined as—"the incremental realization of a worthwhile dream or goal; it's a journey, a way of life, not a destination." They enjoy the present as much as possible, since it's a part of the journey called life! True achievers are constantly developing themselves, their confidence growing as they achieve ever more. (While some have self-confidence in the beginning of their quest, with guidance others can develop it as they go along.) True achievers also have a deep abiding love for people, and give back to society some of what they have to offer.

Winning thoughts attract success, but losing thoughts repel it. It doesn't matter if a person is young or old, short or tall, fat or thin, rich or poor. Race, religion, or ethnicity also has nothing to do with their chances of success either. Successful people are resolute in thinking successful thoughts; they expect to succeed, are committed to succeed, and do whatever it takes to make it happen and succeed. They never give up their quest.

As Winston Churchill so appropriately encouraged his people…

"Never, never, never give in...."

Remember this: It's okay to *feel* like giving in, but it's never okay to actually give in and quit...either on yourself, your family, others you care about, and those who depend on you.

Plan Your Work and Work Your Plan

Now that's certainly a well-worn phrase that most everyone could agree with, at least in principle. However, only 5 to 10 percent of all people actually practice it, while many others may plan but never take the necessary follow-up action. Most people do neither. Here's an example to illustrate...

Bob was an insurance agent in the agency I operated. He always appeared to be highly motivated after every Friday morning sales meeting. He invariably made what seemed to be outstanding plans for the future, and left the office with what appeared to be self-confidence, enthusiasm, and an effective plan. However, Bob's plan never worked. Why? He slept in on Monday morning, failing simply because he didn't carry out his plan. Why? He didn't have the self-motivation to take action, having never developed the habit.

Self-motivated people not only plan their work; they follow through with winning action. Their motivation leads to activation, a key ingredient to success in any endeavor. Winners walk the walk, not just talk the talk. Procrastination causes losing.

I once thought that, as a leader, I was a good motivator. For years I kept getting reasonable results from people with average or below average productivity levels. But while they occasionally achieved outstanding results, what they accomplished overall wasn't acceptable. They were inconsistent in their self-motivation and this led to peaks and valleys in their productivity. I just can't imagine they were happy with their achievement level; I certainly wasn't.

Surround Yourself with People Like YOU Who Want to Succeed

I finally came to realize that if I wanted to accomplish my goals I had better surround myself with self-motivated people, as well as those with the desire to succeed who wanted my guidance in growing and developing themselves to be self-motivated. My attempts at motivating others who lacked desire and were not self-motivated were short-lived. I also learned that striking fear in people's hearts is, at best, a temporary motivator that typically alienates them.

Short-term motivation can be achieved by sharing an inspiring message or stimulating information, focusing on their dream or objective, and instilling a sense of faith and hope by telling them... "You can do it too!" While encouragement is essential for most, sustained motivation comes only from within. It's the missing link which they need to internalize by believing "I *can* do it!" and then proving it to themselves by *actually doing* it!

Your people may get fired up at a weekend function, but unless they augment their belief with a strong internal desire coupled with commitment, they'll fail to follow through on Monday. That's when the true test of working toward what they say they want or are going to do confronts them.

Always set a high level of expectation for both yourself and others, as your winning attitude is key to everyone's success. Create an environment in which everyone can excel.

Become More Self-Motivated and Help Others Do Likewise

If you're someone who's not yet as self-motivated as you'd like to be, the great news is you can change and grow... as long as you have the desire. With perseverance, sacrifice, and commitment, along with a winning attitude and a big dream, you can intensify your self-motivation. Perhaps it's time to prove to yourself that you're serious about taking charge and making it happen.

Anyone can change his or her habits and attitudes; and as previously mentioned it takes only 21 days to accomplish that. Always look at yourself and others as you and they can be, not as you and they currently are. We can all reach higher and become more than we currently are as we work toward fulfilling our potential.

Here are some ideas that can assist anyone to become more self-motivated. These principles are useful not only for your business or career success, but also for your personal life:

- **Build your relationships on mutual trust and respect,** and create win-win situations so everyone benefits.
- **Recognize the potential of others** and the untapped talent they have. If they're willing to develop their skills and abilities and seek your guidance, be sure to help them.
- **Establish a plan for success** by writing down your dreams, including everything you want out of life. Then attach a date to each dream—making each one a goal. You may want to do this with your mentor or leader.
- **Become committed by planning** your course of action and strengthening your willingness to pay the price.

- **Listen and watch others** with whom you're communicating, paying attention to both their verbal and non-verbal cues. Discover what you can learn about them through your observations and ask them questions about what they're saying. Always be honest and sincere. People don't care how much you know until they know how much you care.

- **Use positive reinforcement to help others** build on their strengths, and compliment them as appropriate. Address mistakes with empathy and help others grow through their weaknesses. Be kind, patient, and encouraging.

- **Handle setbacks by constantly focusing on your goals** and dreams and what you're doing to pursue them. Know that a delay isn't a denial...as long as you keep going.

Self-confidence and self-esteem are fundamental qualities of a self-motivated person. Always be the kind of person you'd want as a friend or associate, conducting yourself as though you were someone you'd like to buy from, work with, or do business with.

You Only Have One Chance to Make a Good First Impression!

Effective communication is another important component of self-motivation. You relate to others in both verbal and non-verbal ways. When you're face-to-face your non-verbal communication often gives others their first and possibly most lasting impression. It consists of how you present yourself, including: your mannerisms, grooming, posture, attitude, handshake, facial expression, tone of voice, and eye contact. All of these things need to reflect a winning attitude, which is essential for others to have confidence in and want to associate with or buy from you.

When you shake hands, make sure your grip is firm but not vise-like, and look the person directly in the eye. A weak handshake is considered a sign of weakness ... someone lacking in self-esteem and self-confidence. If you look elsewhere while shaking someone's hand, or later as you're talking with them, it shows a lack of interest in the other person. Focus on them with your full attention, and ignore any potential distractions.

When you look good you generally feel good about yourself. What you wear can make a significant statement of non-verbal communication. It certainly doesn't change your philosophies or ideals, but it can send a winning or losing message. For example, say you're an independent business owner who works from home and used to dressing very casually around the house. However, you've scheduled an appointment to meet with a prospect at a local restaurant and wonder what would be best to wear.

The person you're meeting will be coming from their office, most likely in a suit or nice casual. So, even though you may not want to, it would probably be best to dress up a bit. Too casual an attire could send the prospect a non-verbal message that detracts from your credibility, as well as possibly showing disrespect for them. You may not be taken seriously and be unable to communicate with them as effectively as you'd like, losing out on developing what could have been a long-term customer or associate.

Would your confidence in an attorney you're meeting for the first time be diminished if they were dressed in a tee-shirt, jeans, shorts, or sandals? Now due to various viewpoints, some of you probably said yes while others said no! But think about it.

While a cocktail at lunch may be acceptable in some business circles, it can quickly destroy your chances of success. Most people will lose confidence in you and question your credibility. It doesn't matter how little you drink, it still sends a losing non-verbal sign that can be disastrous in building relationships…so stay away from alcohol! Besides which, it dulls your mental sharpness, which you'll need all of as you make your presentation. Simply have a nice safe cup of coffee, tea, or soda.

Other winning non-verbal signs are clean fingernails, clean and neat hair, a fresh, light scent, no facial hair, and appropriate shoes. Of course, never smoke in anyone's presence. Better yet, don't smoke at all. Besides being harmful to your health, it could be an immediate turnoff to those you're with.

Since enthusiasm and a winning attitude are contagious, always exhibit them in both your non-verbal and verbal communications. They're important parts of having a successful discussion or sharing what you have to offer.

Now if you sit behind a desk you'll appear authoritative, which will alienate some people. To eliminate this risk and really communicate, come out from behind the desk and pull up a chair, so you can participate with them on a more equal person-to-person basis. This generally makes for a more relaxed atmosphere, as you will have eliminated the communication barrier a desk creates. It's likely your visitor will be more at ease and therefore more open to your thoughts, suggestions, products, services, or opportunity.

Tips for Raising Self-Confidence, Self-Esteem, and Self-Motivation

1. **Act and be enthusiastic** … and by all means smile! Walk with purpose even if you're only going for a cup of coffee. Always maintain excellent posture while sitting, standing, and walking.

2. **Energize your voice,** while improving your listening skills, memory, routine, and everything else needing fine-tuning that affects your life and interpersonal relationships.

3. **Get things done** … particularly important things you may have been putting off … that will help you achieve your dreams and goals. For example, reach out and keep in touch with everyone on your prospect or customer list! A sense of accomplishment helps to improve your outlook. To catch up start your daily tasks earlier than normal so you can work on and complete lingering projects.

4. **Always speak in winning terms,** while encouraging your associates to do the same. An enthusiastic solution-and-possibility-oriented attitude and behavior can accomplish what a pessimistic, problem-focused, apathetic attitude and behavior never will!

5. **Consistently learn more about what you're doing** and upgrade your skills, whether it's product knowledge, leadership, or something else. Maintain the thought that you'll be a better leader, next week or next month, than you are today. Knowledge can help you improve your performance and self-confidence. Keep practicing what's yours to do. Always be learning and growing.

6. **Develop the level of self-esteem** that comes from focusing on your dreams, setting goals, and doing whatever it takes to reach them. Make them challenging, forcing yourself to stretch and grow in the quest. Reset your goals as often as necessary to achieve them, and never quit on yourself or anyone else who's counting on you for leadership.

7. **As a leader, people are watching you and what you do!** Your attitude will take on more of a winning posture when you have something specific you're striving for. It's energizing to yourself and others.

Self-motivation leads to actions and, therefore, results … which can be winning or losing, depending on the purpose. Let's say it's to watch TV, which is an advertising medium to get viewers to buy things they probably don't need or really can't afford. "Riding" the couch or recliner until it "dies," their losing behavior results in wasting precious time they could otherwise invest in getting ahead. It's a losing distraction, a temporary pleasure or escape that, especially if it becomes a habit, keeps viewers stuck from *ever* living the better life they say they really want. It takes them off track!

However, being self-motivated with a winning purpose leads to winning actions, which require you to always do your best … and then better it! You may or may not get the results you want. If for some reason you don't, reflect on your self-motivation and actions, improve on them, and go for the results you want. Learn from the situation, and keep moving forward more smartly.

Truly Successful People Are Humble, Self-Motivated, and Self-Disciplined…Gaining Wisdom as They Go and Grow

Humility knows that no one can accomplish very much alone, giving credit where it's due; whereas ego brags and takes all the credit. As shared earlier, people don't care how much you know until they know how much you care. Humility breeds caring respectful people who are essential for building long-lasting mutually beneficial relationships, personally and professionally.

Realize that everyone makes mistakes … no one is perfect. Mistakes are just events; they're not who you are. Forgive yourself and keep going. Humility helps you stay grounded and on a winning track after you've made mistakes or failed in some way. It's essential for achieving the measure of success, happiness, and meaning you want in life.

Important note: Achievements resulting from illegal, immoral, or unethical means have no place in the life of a truly successful person or anyone aspiring to be so. Anyone who forgoes good values in order to accomplish something will always suffer for it. It's just not worth it. Never give in to any temptation to shortcut the challenging but tremendously worthwhile process of success.

Humility is essential, especially when you accomplish major goals that put you in the limelight. As others are congratulating you, it takes true humility to appropriately acknowledge the role certain people played in your victory … and be grateful for it. Whenever you're recognized for an accomplishment it's tempting to just bask in the glow of admiration, but don't be enamored with yourself or think you're better than anyone else. Nobody's a big deal!

It's important to share the glory—giving credit where credit is due. How much did you, as an individual, really put into this effort? Does some or even much of the credit belong to others, for example: your spouse, children, friends, employees, co-workers, associates, mentor, or leaders? If so, acknowledge certain of these people as appropriate. Thank the people who guided, supported, and helped you, and they'll be likely to want to help you achieve even more.

Wisdom is having a true understanding of people and life. It's being a clear thinker with an excellent sense of what's going on and the ability and courage to make sound decisions. It's also having good common sense, which actually seems to be uncommon! It's simply perception and reasoning while using good judgment.

Self-motivated people who are successful long-term have developed the wisdom to make sound decisions based on common sense, experience, and what they've learned. This wisdom comes both by their own trial and error and what they learn from others personally, as well as from books and audios. They also have an understanding of and appreciation for the winning factors that influence their lives. They take nothing and no one for granted.

Self-discipline is following through with what you have promised yourself in a specific area, such as: time/activity management, including...not wasting time on losing activities; living a fine values-based life; staying committed to your goals; doing whatever it takes to succeed; sticking to your heart-healthy diet; and adhering to the exercise program you know will improve your attitude, reduce stress, and give you a healthier body and more alert mind.

Being self-disciplined allows you to do things that are really important to you and your success. You deliberately block out time to do what you need to do to achieve your goals, and actually *do* it. As a reward for accomplishing goals, from time-to-time you can blend in some fun activities without feeling guilty. You're not wasting time on activities that distract you from working toward your objectives, and you don't procrastinate taking winning actions. As a result, you do more of what really matters to you and your family.

Self-discipline is having a plan—an agenda with a definite purpose—and a solid commitment to take action in following that plan so you can reach your goals. It's deferring instant gratification to attain a dream or goal. For instance, you may prefer to watch TV or shop, but you promised yourself, and perhaps your family, that you'd build your business or career. So you invest your time wisely to fulfill the promise.

Self-discipline is a prerequisite for self-motivation. Practice it, improve it, and live it—walk your talk—to accomplish your goals and dreams. And while you're doing that, you stick to fine values.

If you have any weakness in any of these characteristics ... humility, self-motivation, self-discipline, and wisdom...work hard to focus on and strengthen them.

In the past, have you ever blamed things like a poor home environment, inadequate education, or an absence of direction for any lack of self-motivation you may have? The great news is it can be rejuvenated by taking total responsibility for everything in your life. You past doesn't create your future; it's your thinking and actions going forward that do. Learn from the past, let it go, and move on!

Shift your focus, and take corrective action by thinking only winning thoughts. Keep taking winning actions so you can achieve the results and the success you want. Then keep setting bigger goals so you can achieve even bigger dreams, thereby preparing yourself for ever-increasing success...and happiness.

As playwright and director Moss Hart shared about some of the benefits of success...

> *"Can success change the human mechanism so completely between one dawn and another? Can it make one feel taller, more alive, handsomer [or prettier], uncommonly gifted, and indomitably secure with the certainty that this is the way life will always be? Yes it can and it does!"*

Use your self-motivation to activate yourself in doing what it takes to grow and achieve more of what's important to you. This will not only enrich your personal life, but also enhance your success in getting ahead in your business or career, while bringing you greater happiness and a more meaningful life. It's what leaders and other achievers do around the world. Pave the road to your dreams and goals with your own relentless self-motivation.

Those who invest in personal development as part of their ongoing training and education can grow into becoming the person they were created to be, more capable of evolving into the "shareperson" and leader they'd like to be.

This means understanding, believing in, and caring about others... such as prospects, customers, and business associates... as well as in sharing their products, services, and opportunity, and how they can best serve.

In addition, they're constantly treating others in such a way that they're trusted and known for their integrity.

—5—

Could *Sharing* Be the Ultimate Key to Success?

"Three keys to more abundant living: caring about others, daring for others, sharing with others."—William Arthur Ward

KEEP ON SHARING! No matter what you're aiming for in life…constantly network, extend the hand of friendship, and share what you have to offer. If you just keep it all to yourself, you won't help anyone and you'll never succeed!

You may have been the one who shared the idea with your spouse of spending the rest of your life together in marriage. As you grew up, it's likely you shared your feelings and dreams with your parents; and you undoubtedly shared your capabilities, enthusiasm, and desire to work for your employer during the interview.

You may have shared a business concept with others and they decided to join you as an independent business owner associate. Since sharing is such an integral part of life, make the most of your life by sharpening your sharing skills. This, along with a winning attitude, will enable you to reach higher goals and live your dream.

The "KASH" Principle

Early in my career, I learned an acronym—KASH—that played a key role in my development as a top salesman, sales manager, and leader in my profession. It also helped me throughout my involvement in various civic, charitable, church, and business associations, and it can help you in building your business or profession.

Over the years, much study, research, and observation has been devoted to identifying and developing the techniques of truly successful people, who are all good at *sharing* ideas and building relationships. The KASH Principle highlights key elements necessary for success:

- **K** is for knowledge
- **A** is for attitude
- **S** is for skills
- **H** is for habits

While all are important, one is absolutely decisive. Which one is it? Let's take a look…

Share Your KNOWLEDGE with Enthusiasm

Knowledge can be acquired by most anyone, given enough time. There are countless how-to books written to assist you in gaining knowledge of anything you want to learn. Unfortunately, there are some people who make their product, service, or opportunity appear to be complicated. They apparently do this to impress a customer or prospect with their knowledge. But as you may have discovered, this approach simply doesn't work. Keep things simple and you and everyone else will be better off.

I recall going on a group interview some years ago with a regional group insurance representative. We made our presentation by showing the prospective client how our product would solve his problem: providing adequate life and health coverage to his employees at a reasonable cost to his company.

Our solution conformed to their needs and we made the proposal easy for the client to understand. He purchased our plan and then confided to us that he had been shopping around for some time. He shared that salespeople from other insurance companies had made the solution appear complicated and quite confusing, to the point where it looked problematic. Therefore, since he couldn't understand it, he refused to buy it.

This reminds me of the well-known "KISS" principle: Keep It Simple and Straightforward. You can't go wrong by using this approach in dealing with others.

Knowledge is power, but only when it's shared and can be put to use. If it's kept dormant, it's of absolutely no value. Knowledge can't do anything until it's shared.

As an analogy, consider a vehicle's engine. With fuel it can produce power, but it's of absolutely no value unless a small but consequential universal joint connects it to and shares it with the drive shaft. When it does, the wheels turn, the vehicle moves forward, and the driver can get to where he or she wants to go.

For you, knowledge is the engine. With enthusiasm it can produce power. But until you, the universal joint, share what you've learned in your business or career with others, it's of absolutely no value. You can make progress only when you share. This is the only way you can get to where you want to go along the road of success.

Put Your SKILLS into Action

Skills can be developed or acquired by training and experience, then sharpened by continual use. You can learn what you need to know professionally through books, audios, videos, seminars, trainings, and online resources. You'll gain a deeper understanding of it all and be able to more effectively share it with others, including not only facts and figures, but also technical and people skills.

If you don't pay attention and learn to understand and develop empathy, however, and you focus only on the cold hard facts without considering the needs and desires of your prospects, customers, and associates few will accept what you share. Since most people make decisions based primarily on emotion, backed up by some degree of logic, they'll ultimately do something only if they have a strong enough reason to.

Skill is the ability to successfully use the knowledge acquired. Understanding and discernment are needed to make intelligent use of it, which comes with observation and experience. There are basic human wants and needs that influence most people's decisions, making it essential to do your best in understanding people. You can then share how your product, service, or opportunity can fulfill their wants and needs while, at the same time, providing them with a solution they may have been looking for. Perhaps you could even show them a way to get ahead. No matter what, though, always strive for excellence as you practice your skills, caring about others.

As Helen Keller experienced…

> *"When we do the best we can, we never know what miracle is wrought in our life or in the lives of others. Alone we can do so little; together we can do so much!"*

HABITS Are Like Putting Certain Behaviors on Autopilot

We're all creatures of habit; some habits help us win while others only lead to losing. Fortunately, as discussed before, we can change our habits through deliberate conscious effort applied over time. Habits require little or no conscious thought once they become "embedded" into your subconscious mind. They're like an autopilot, which is great as long as they are winning beneficial habits. While lots of people possess three elements of the "KASH" Principle—Knowledge, Skills, and Habits—truly successful people also have…

The Most Decisive Ingredient Is ATTITUDE!

Whatever your career or business, a winning attitude is necessary for success; a losing attitude guarantees failure! Since business, as well as life, is built largely on relationships, those with a losing attitude…no matter how great their Knowledge, Skills, or Habits…can't possibly win with others, succeed, and be happy.

For example, truckers, waitpersons, teachers, executives, independent business owners, bank tellers, homemakers, parents, police, salespeople, and all others need to maintain a winning attitude in order to have favorable results in their lives. This may seem obvious but, amazingly, a lot of people simply don't get it. They keep dumping losing ideas on others, not realizing the no-win self-fulfilling prophecy they're promoting. Then when they don't win, they blame someone or something else.

Realize it or not we're all in "sales," revealing ourselves by our attitude and how we treat others. A person with a winning attitude takes an interest in others, who they are, what they're going through, their hopes and dreams. We often have the chance to either "sell" ourselves to others, or lose the "sale" by not taking an interest in them. When we care enough to uplift and encourage others we're more likely to achieve rapport and the potential for a friendship, which could lead to a customer or associate relationship.

Since a winning attitude is essential in all we do, here's a list of six ideas fundamental to your success and happiness … regardless of your primary or secondary occupation:

1. **Maintain a winning attitude toward the fields** you've chosen for your job and/or business. Sure you may want to make a career change, and that's great! But in the meantime, it's important to do your best in looking for the good and to be pleasant for your own sake, as well as for the well-being of those around you.

2. **Maintain a winning attitude toward the products,** services, or opportunity you have to share, and have complete confidence in their value. If you don't believe in what you're sharing, how can you reasonably expect your customers, prospects, and associates to believe that you can help them solve a problem, let alone realize a dream?

Your own use of the products and services you offer can go a long way in bolstering your belief in them, as well as setting an example for others to believe in them too. It's the best way you can honestly recommend something to others. Your personal experience can make a big difference.

If you're offering a product you don't use, like wheelchairs, you can boost your credibility by talking with people who have or are successfully using the product and have glowing comments about it that you can share with others.

3. **Maintain a winning attitude toward your company,** organization, and the leaders with whom you're connected. Believe you're associated with the best company and organization in the industry, and that your leaders can lead you in the direction you need to go to reach your goals.

4. **Maintain a winning attitude toward yourself,** recognizing and appreciating the self-confidence, self-esteem, and empathy you've developed so far. How can you appreciate, respect, and care about others if you don't respect, appreciate, and care about yourself? You can't give or share with other people what you don't already have.

5. **Maintain a winning attitude toward those who may need** or want what you have to offer, that it's desirable and in demand, and that they're open to considering it.

6. **Maintain a winning attitude toward helping others.** Have and show a sincere interest in their well-being, demonstrating your other-centeredness toward them. Since a winning attitude is contagious; therefore, those you come in contact with can be uplifted and encouraged by your attitude and enthusiasm, regardless of their response to what you're sharing.

Be a Friend...Help Others by *Sharing* What You Have to Offer!

While everyone loves to buy or get in on a good thing or opportunity, no one likes to be "sold" or taken advantage of. This is easy to understand as many believe salespeople typically try to convince or manipulate others into doing something they don't want to do, or push them into buying something they neither need, want, nor can afford...or simply aren't interested in.

If you were to push someone into saying "yes" to something you're offering based on *your* reasons or goals they'll probably end up unhappy and may even resent you for it. It's always best when people say "yes" for *their* reasons or goals, not yours! As success and relationship guru Dale Carnegie observed...

"Those convinced against their will are of the same opinion still."

Even though selling is among the world's highest paid professions, anyone with a negative opinion of it goes on the defensive. Unfortunately, they don't give themselves the chance to realize that in its most honorable caring form it's simply about *sharing*.

When you sincerely *share* what you have to offer—be it a product, service, opportunity, or idea—with others, they're more likely to feel that you're presenting a solution to one or more of their wants, needs, or challenges. Or it could be something to help them avoid a problem in the future, a preventive measure. Share with them in as nice a no-pressure way as you can...just as a friend would!

As the sage advice goes...

"If you want a friend you first need to be a friend"!

When you share with someone what you have to offer, you're presenting something for them to consider. You want your prospect, customer, or client to understand how what you're sharing could help them make their life more enjoyable, overcome an obstacle, or perhaps realize a goal or a dream. Sharing offers *no pressure.*

Discover the other person's real need or desire by asking them questions, listening carefully to what they have to say. Focus on how you can help them get what they want or need. If you don't have it then maybe you could suggest someone else who may be able to help them. It's all part of honestly caring about others. Beyond that, you could suggest that if they know someone who might be able to benefit from what you're sharing you'd be happy to help them.

Since we're basically emotional creatures, many make decisions backed up only somewhat by logic, while others are more detail oriented. But no matter how great what you have to share is nobody will even consider buying from or associating with you without having a strong enough reason—a *why*—to do so. So focus on their "why."

Regardless of a prospect's detail orientation, when they start asking questions that's a sign of interest, or they wouldn't bother to ask! This is your chance to add value and start building a relationship ... addressing their questions and concerns, supplying useful information, and explaining details. Interacting directly with prospects is key to success, while doing so through social media is called "social selling." It's using social media productively rather than for engaging in communications that can't get you anywhere.

Once your prospect, customer, or client gets excited about the results they could get, or achieve, with what you're sharing they're more likely to move in your direction. They'll be more inclined to take advantage of what you have to offer when they realize you can help them get what they want or need. That person needs to have a desire they want to fulfill, perhaps a dream or goal, before you can realistically expect them to go forward with your offering.

Adopt a "Shareperson" Attitude and Sociably Share Solutions!

If you're anxious and try to "push" someone into buying something or associating with you, you'll surely alienate and push them away. How about thinking of yourself as a "shareperson," attentively sharing solutions to others' wants, needs, dreams, goals, and objectives in a friendly sociable way? This attitude increases your chances of relating with them and their wanting your solutions.

Reaching out most effectively in order to serve others via your business or profession may well be called "sharepersonship," which could be defined as—

> "extending the hand of friendship, taking a sincere interest in others, building rapport, as you begin understanding them and their situation. It's caring enough to offer, as may be appropriate, getting together so you can discover their wants, needs, goals, dreams, or objectives, then sharing in a friendly sociable way what you have to offer that could help them."

It could be a solution to a personal care, beauty, weight, health and wellness, or household need or problem...and even a practical way to help them get ahead and live a better life. Sharepersonship could also be thought of as "a sociable way to success," an approach you can use to meet people and build relationships. Depending on their wants, needs, dreams, or objectives you could potentially share your product(s), service(s), or opportunity with them as appropriate.

While electronic tools make communications faster and easier, to develop a successful business or career it's essential to build and maintain excellent relationships. Care sincerely for those who associate with or buy from you, and others you come in contact with, always thinking kindly of them and their well-being and what you can do to best serve or help them, thereby strengthening your relationships. It's central to what makes for a thriving business or career.

Even though social media is a great tool with which to leverage in growing a business or career, anyone who tries to avoid the relationship-building process, as challenging as that may be, will limit their potential and fail to serve or help others as well as they otherwise could have. They'll both miss out on what could have led to a great friendship and possibly a great business relationship or enterprise.

However capable we may be, to move forward in life we need to keep learning and growing as people, while treating others with kindness. It's human nature for all of us to want life to be easy, and we'd like everyone to be a joy to deal with. But part of growing and succeeding is a result of consistently being considerate of others, whether they're always likeable or not.

No matter how you go about building your career or business... YOU're the "magic"! With a "shareperson" attitude you caringly communicate and work with others in creating mutually beneficial relationships, which is key to success, happiness, and meaning.

Leaders Empower People and Manage Things

The greatest responsibility of leaders is to those they lead and serve. Excellent leaders and parents have the values and character traits that upgrade the quality of life for those they affect. Here are several traits appropriate for leaders in all areas:

- **Above all,** maintain a winning attitude as it provides an environment for winning thoughts. This, in turn, sets the stage for taking winning actions, which, when done, are more likely to bring about winning results. It's a chain reaction.

- **Care enough to inspire,** encourage, and empower others, while challenging them to reach for their potential.

- **Be enthusiastic about opening your mind** so discovery and learning can take place. It's contagious and can make prospecting, sharing, and other communications and relationship building smoother, more effective, and more fun.

- **Use creativity and imagination in going beyond** the humdrum, keeping you and your followers excited about what's happening. Great leaders are just ordinary people doing extraordinary things.

- **Be willing and able to do whatever it takes** with the self-discipline to follow through. Example is the best teacher.

- **Develop and maintain a sound mind and body.** Keep fit with a heart-healthy diet and exercise program that will provide you with the energy and stamina you need to positively influence others by your excellent example of looking good and feeling good.

- **Use challenges to build character,** courage, and integrity. That's how those three are developed. No excuses!

- **Be trustworthy by keeping your promises** and agreements. No "shortchanging" allowed. If necessary, renegotiate if changes to them would best serve.

- **Be a good communicator by truly listening to others,** recognizing, and responding to both their verbal and non-verbal communications.

- **Treat others as you would have them treat you**...with appreciation, respect, fairness, and dignity.

- **Rather than blaming others, accept responsibility** for your actions and shortcomings...and improve upon them.

- **Maintain a forgiving attitude** toward yourself and others by giving yourself and them the benefit of the doubt. Otherwise you'll be hurting yourself as you carry around old "baggage." Forgive yourself...for your own peace of mind.

- **Maintain a strong belief in the potential of others.** This nurtures self-confidence and self-esteem in your business or career associates, family, friends, and others with whom you have an opportunity to make a positive difference.

- **Treat everyone as an individual** who has his or her own wants, needs, dreams, and goals. They may be totally different then yours, but that's what individuality is all about. We all have something to offer.

- **Always complete important tasks before** they become urgent. Focus on your priorities in line with your purpose, delegating as necessary.

How to Be an Effective Communicator

To successfully share an idea, principle, value, or something else...with a prospect, customer, spouse, son or daughter, friend, or others you talk with...requires being an effective communicator.

Your perception of a given situation, idea, or person, and your sincerity influences your ability to communicate as a leader. Avoid giving the prideful impression that says you know all the answers and you're always right. Be humble. No one is perfect no matter how intelligent or experienced they may be. There's always something to learn.

A winning flexible attitude and behavior are essential in creating open, clear, and effective communications. For example, this includes: caring, sincerity, fairness, open-mindedness, listening to understand, speaking to be understood, and not speaking down to others. Status, or looking down on someone, has no place in the life of a winning-attitude leader. You might even think of a person with status as—someone who buys something they can't afford to impress someone they don't like who probably doesn't care anyway!

When you communicate, offer your opinion as you understand the situation to be. Then ask for input and ideas from others, allowing them the opportunity to participate by sharing their unique perspectives and recommendations about the potential solution(s).

Effective communication requires effort; it doesn't just automatically happen. Certain skills are needed and through practice, we can master and perfect them. For example, good authors rewrite their manuscripts over and over again until they get them just so. So, it follows that the secret to effective communicative writing is rewriting, including emails and texts! Why, then, wouldn't fine-tuning verbal communication skills be to our advantage? Makes sense, doesn't it?

Since mutual understanding is key to effective communication, we need to say what we mean and mean what we say. Otherwise, our communications will be hindered...to say the least. Listening is also essential for mutual understanding. Unless you hear and understand what the other person is saying effective communication is impossible. Listening involves patience, openness, empathy, and a sincere desire to understand what's being said.

Here's What Can Happen if You Don't Truly Listen

I recall an example of a salesman, we'll call him Joe, who didn't listen to his prospect, a businessman we'll call George, and almost lost the sale. I had accompanied Joe to propose a large amount of insurance to George so he could fund an agreement to dispose of his business in the event of his death or disability.

After Joe had made an effective presentation, George started asking what he considered an important question that Joe thought was only a minor detail. So, instead of allowing George to finish his question, Joe anticipated what he thought George was going to say, interrupted, and gave a response that had nothing to do with the question. George, again, tried to ask the same question, but Joe still interrupted, offering an irrelevant response.

I could sense George's building frustration, so I interjected, "Joe, let's allow George to finish his question." After we both listened to his real concern, we were able to respond and satisfy it with ease, and the sale was immediately closed!

The trap of not truly listening to the statements, ideas, concerns, or questions of the prospect, associate, customer, or client can damage or be fatal to a relationship, not only professionally but also personally. Listen fully so you can ask germane and meaningful questions to gain a deeper understanding of the other person.

To better earn the confidence and trust of others, you need to sharpen your listening skills, ask appropriate questions, and show your honesty, integrity, and kindness…all key ingredients to building and maintaining winning relationships. They need to know you care about them, their needs, and wants. Listening attentively lays the foundation for a quality relationship. You can have many fine values and characteristics, and be as "pure as the driven snow," but if you don't listen to what others have to say, you can't help them.

Time and time again, poor listening skills get people in trouble! You can only gain and sustain another's confidence and trust by being consistently interested in them, their well-being, and helping them. Sincerely walk your talk in the process and, by your outstanding example, show others how to listen well.

How Well Do You Understand Non-Verbal Communication?

As we covered briefly earlier, a leader needs to be knowledgeable in non-verbal as well as verbal messages. Body position and movements, as well as voice volume and tone modulation, are significant in understanding non-verbal communication.

Whether we're consciously doing it or not, we all use non-verbal methods in conveying our feelings and thoughts. For example, here are a few of them:

- **Next to your voice, your eyes are** your most powerful communicators. Eye contact is crucial when speaking with someone because it conveys interest, sincerity, confidence, concern, and trust. Lack of eye contact shows a lack of interest, sincerity, confidence, concern, and trust, which begs the question, "Do you really mean what you're saying?"

- **Your face is the most expressive part of your body,** including if it displays a deadpan look! Your facial expressions communicate your feelings quite noticeably. It's highly likely that through them you most reveal your feelings of interest, excitement, surprise, joy, thankfulness, anger, fear, sadness, or disinterest.

- **A genuine smile ☺ conveys delight and warm feelings,** but a forced smile comes across as fake; just showing your teeth isn't enough! Reflect interest and gladness in being with the other person by engaging your face in a broad genuine smile. Your eyes sparkle, your mouth opens, widens, and curves upward on both sides. It tells the other person that you accept and are happy to see them, while having a winning positive effect on you as well. It's a gift you give yourself, as well as to your recipient(s) ... making it more likely that they'll be open to what you have to offer.

    Now you may be laughing at the detailed description. But have you ever seen anyone whose expression was so firmly set in a frown, a look of boredom, that you almost expected their face to "crack" if they were to "shock" it with a smile? Or how about those who flash their teeth because they believe they must, rather than give a sincere smile? That's why the art of smiling is so thoroughly described here, especially for those who have yet to master it.

- **The ability to read body posture** enables you to determine generally how others feel, as well as what you're projecting to them if you carry that same posture. When they stand straight with relaxed but squared shoulders, perhaps with their hands positioned behind their back, that's a sign of confidence and strength. If they're seated and leaning forward it's a sign of interest and confidence. If shoulders are drooped, it's usually a sign of being self-conscious, guilty, and fearful, as well as being burdened, feeling like a victim, or lacking self-confidence and self-esteem.

    When someone folds their arms across their chest it conveys a lack of interest and a closed mind, even if it's done just because they're cold or tired. If they do so when standing they can also come across as arrogant, thinking they're better than others. So an open body posture is best.

- **People broadcast their thoughts through** various gestures. For example, in the US thumbs-up indicates a job well done; a "high five" with touching vertically outstretched palms is for victory or a good deed; a raised clenched fist pumping the air can be a sign of cheering someone on or a indication of being fired up; nodding the head indicates acceptance; and a raised index finger signifies the person or organization is number one. (If you travel internationally be aware. An innocent positive gesture in one country could be a rude gesture in another. Learn about the culture's gestures or you could ruin a relationship before it has a chance to get started!)

- **Many of us have non-verbal habits we don't realize** may be distracting and indicate nervousness. Habits like jingling of pocket coins, repeated clicking of a ballpoint pen, picking at or biting nails, "cracking" knuckles, tapping a pen or fingers on a table or desk, wringing or clenching of hands, and constantly checking the phone.

- **Remember to use a firm, but not bone-crushing,** handshake with eye contact. Together they communicate confidence and interest. While shaking hands is common, it isn't universally practiced. In the US it's often used when meeting, greeting, or congratulating someone, creating a connection. Now when it comes to men and women shaking hands, the woman would offer her hand first, the man holding back to see if she does.

Review your own non-verbal cues and fine-tune them so you're supporting rather than taking away from the effectiveness of your communications. Always be alert to the non-verbal signs from others so you can appropriately respond to their needs and concerns. It can pay big dividends!

Are You Planning to Succeed?

Planning is essential in order to effectively use your time and maximize results. The key, however, is *flexible* planning. If your plans have no flexibility, you may be wasting your valuable time going nowhere if something doesn't go exactly according to plan. "So what could go wrong with a well-developed plan?" you ask.

- **You experience a "no-show"** whereby a prospect or customer forgets they have an appointment with you, or they changed their mind and didn't have the courtesy to tell you.

- **A prospect or customer cancels** or reschedules their appointment with you.

- **You have a situation requiring** your immediate attention that comes up in your family, job, or business that precludes following your plan.

Flexible planning helps you work around the unexpected. From your past experiences, you know such things are bound to happen. Things don't always go exactly as planned. It's impossible to anticipate and plan for every possible challenge that might present itself. When things don't go as expected, don't let it bother you. Maintain a winning attitude, learn from it, adjust for it, and move on.

You want to maximize your productivity, right? Of course! Then make as many appointments as you can fit into your schedule—stay booked. If one happens to be a no-show, gets canceled, or needs rescheduled, you can still make progress by scheduling another appointment and/or doing something else with that time that can contribute to the growth of your business.

Being heavily scheduled indicates that you're going for it, and a lot of people want to get together with you. You're taking charge of your business...making things happen...rather than just being a victim of someone who has canceled on you or doesn't show up. As a winner, you consider any break in the action a benefit that allows you to get something else important done during that time.

If you're going to be running late for an appointment, a phone call or text would be considerate and appreciated. People respect and enjoy doing business with enthusiastically productive people like YOU! You're a winner who gets things done, using your time wisely for your own maximum benefit, as well as that of others who you're endeavoring to serve.

More Tips on Achieving Top-Notch Sales/Sharing Performance

Confirming what was shared earlier, Bill Gove, the father of professional speaking and renowned sales consultant, said, contrary to popular belief, "Selling is not talking someone into doing something he or she doesn't want to do. People like to buy. Selling then is making it easy for them to do what they enjoy doing. Sure the professional salesperson gives the prospect reasons why it's better to buy now than it is to delay, but they make sure that the reasons they give are the prospect's not theirs."

Gove shared three things that are also quite applicable to those who share products or services, as well as for those who are also building an organization of independent business owners:

1. **Build growing relationships.** Establish yourself as a problem solver by understanding your prospect's or customer's wants and needs. Keep your presentation on track and respect their time and opinions.

2. **Make it easy for the prospect or customer to act** by helping them arrive at their own decision. Reassure them that their decision is rational by direct and indirect suggestion.

3. **Help them recognize and remove any obstacles** that stand in the way, like: (A) Delay: "I'll have to think about it"; (B) Time or money: "I don't have the time or money"; or (C) Resistance to change: "I'm satisfied with the way things are."

The Story of the Hot Dog Vendor

There once was a man who lived by the side of the road and offered delicious hot dogs. He put up signs and advertised in the newspaper sharing how tasty and nutritious they were.

Enthusiastic, he'd shout, "Step right up for a great hot dog right here, right now…you'll love it!" People from all over stopped, smiled, and bought them in droves. The man increased his meat, bun, condiment, and soda orders, and built a bigger stand to take care of his growing business.

Things were going so well that he convinced his son, who was home from college, to join him in expanding the business. But before too long, his son, rather than applauding and supporting his father, dampened his spirits by presenting him with the losing perspective he had bought into: "Father, haven't you been listening to the radio and watching TV? There's a big recession going on; the foreign situation is terrible and the domestic one is even worse. You can't possibly continue succeeding in business. Better shut down now and try to get your old job down at the docks back."

Whereupon the father thought, "Well, my son's been to college, so he ought to know what's going on." Allowing his nay-saying son to discourage him, the father canceled his order for supplies, took down his signs, canceled his ads, and no longer bothered to stand by the side of the road to offer his hotdogs. From then on everyone saw that he had gone out of business, and were disappointed they could no longer enjoy his uplifting attitude and great hot dogs!

The father then lamented, "You were right, son. We're definitely in a big recession. As much as I love being in my own business, I guess I'll have to try to get my old job back, which aggravates me no end. But I've got to pay the bills. What a bummer!" (He had created his own "personal recession" by blindly adopting his son's losing attitude. Never let naysayers dissuade you from moving forward!)

A week later a former customer who wanted to be in his own business, opened up a hot dog stand just a hundred feet away. As things developed, he ended up building a huge enterprise with his wife and children, having stands located throughout the area.

The Fine People Who Share and Are Devoted to Helping Others

These people are to be celebrated because of all the good they do for so many. After all, where would we be without them? We'd make virtually no progress nor conduct much commerce, would we? These committed people provide products, services, and opportunities that help countless others in innumerable ways.

To maximize their ability to get ahead and make a bigger difference, they engage daily in personal development as part of their training and education, becoming the person they were created to be, more capable of evolving into the "shareperson" and leader they'd like to be. This means understanding, believing in, and caring about others...such as prospects, customers, and business associates...as well as in sharing their products, services, and opportunity, and how they can best serve. In addition, they're constantly treating others in such a way that they're trusted and known for their integrity.

Those in the selling/sharing arena succeed or fail financially in relation to the business volume they generate. They can't get by on credibility and reputation alone; consistent, productive effort is also required. They're not paid for the hours they work; they get paid for results. Results...and results only...can pay their bills, increase their standard of living, provide for the future of themselves and their families, and make an even bigger difference.

Being a shareperson, whether in your own business or not, offers you an opportunity to earn an income that relates directly to your attitude, effort, and results. To take full advantage of your potential for success, always be looking for potential customers; and if you're also building an organization of associates, always be on the lookout for those who want to get ahead or simply want more happiness and meaning out of life. Be ready to share what you have to offer and help whoever expresses an interest.

Are you moving forward as quickly as you'd like? Most people would say, "No!"

While the process does take time, it can be accelerated by identifying and eliminating any losing beliefs and limitations we've adopted that have caused us to slow or even halt our progress.

Unfortunately, surveys indicate that a vast majority of people tend to look at where they are as being as far as they'll ever go, not recognizing their potential, settling for a not-so-happy status quo.

No wonder so many people are emotionally dead before they even reach 30, only to live the rest of their lives with their dreams forever locked inside, their song unsung.

—6—

How Could You Move Forward More Quickly?

"Experiment! Meet new people. You'll find the unexpected everywhere as you go through life. By adventuring about you become accustomed to the unexpected, which then becomes what it really is...the inevitable." —Amelia Earhart

THERE ARE PEOPLE EVERYWHERE who are in need of and looking for excellent products, services, or an opportunity, and they can be found simply by meeting new people.

With a winning attitude you know you can help others, and the more people you meet, befriend, and share what you have to offer, the more momentum you can gain in moving toward realizing your dreams and goals.

But if you have a losing attitude, you'll only look at prospects as problems rather than opportunities to grow yourself and expand business. So always be upgrading your knowledge and skills, giving your best toward cultivating and making the most of the opportunities you have to build your career or business with those who come across your path every day.

You may have but a minute to meet a new person...who could turn out to be the best prospect you've ever had. Make the most of these golden opportunities to begin what could develop into fruitful relationships. Be proactive. Seize the moment!

Blocked by their own perceived limitations, some people don't look at others as they could be—perhaps an excellent customer or associate. Alertness to such possibilities can help you break through any fear and take advantage of the moment you're given to strike up a conversation that could lead to a mutually beneficial outcome, even a great lifelong friendship. No one can have too many friends; they're good for the soul.

Remember, limitations are self-imposed. Until they're recognized for what they are, falsehoods, and removed, it won't be possible for you to see and use the many opportunities you have for meeting new people that present themselves every day. This is central to moving ahead with focus and commitment.

Utilizing those golden opportunities to reach out to others will make the journey to your dream more exciting and can also shorten the time it'll take for you to reach your objective.

What Losing Beliefs Could Be Limiting You?

Are you moving forward as quickly as you'd like? Most would say, "No!" While the process does take time, it can be accelerated by identifying and eliminating any losing beliefs we've adopted that have caused us to slow or even halt our progress. It's what's inside you that counts most. As Ralph Waldo Emerson proclaimed...

> *"What lies behind you and what lies before you are tiny matters compared to what lies within you."*

Here's a list of beliefs that may be hampering the growth you desire...along with some ideas to help you take winning action:

- **Believing the lack of a college degree or other education is preventing you from succeeding.** Many successful people are actually self-taught—they weren't formally educated in their field. While necessary for certain occupations, specialized training or a college degree, in and of itself, doesn't guarantee success. Whether you have a degree or not, it's having a winning attitude and consistently applying yourself toward achieving your objective that counts most. So get out there and make it happen, learning and growing as you go.

- **Believing it's costly to start a business.** Not necessarily! Many businesses can be started at home on the side for very minimal expense, while you keep working your job.

- **Believing you can't acquire the knowledge or skills to succeed, especially with people.** Learning the particulars of what you're offering, and understanding and skillfully working with people can be done through available continuing non-formal education. You can also learn by observing your mentor or leader, as well as through your own experiences. Some of the best lessons come simply by observing others' attitudes and behaviors, how they affect you, and then *not* doing to others what has affected *you* in a losing way.

- **Believing you don't need an action plan.** The truth is you do. Get with your leader or mentor if you need help in making yours.

- **Believing you don't have time.** We all have 24 hours a day. While you can't control time, per se, you can manage your activities to make the most profitable use of your time.

- **Believing you can't increase your self-confidence and self-esteem.** Fortunately, action cures fear and builds confidence and self-esteem. So take charge and overcome the obstacles as you work toward achieving your goals.

- **Believing negative experiences hold you back.** Instead, always ask yourself, "What can I learn from this experience so I can do better and keep going…stronger than ever?"

- **Believing you can't have a more winning attitude.** We all need to monitor our attitude and upgrade it, as necessary, throughout each day. Everyone has room for improvement.

After carefully reviewing any losing beliefs you may have been holding on to, limiting your progress, let them go by embracing the truth and taking winning action. This eliminates their hold-back effect on your business or profession, and well worth the time and effort it takes to achieve, as it's essential for moving forward,

You may need to adjust your thinking or goals, and even change your career focus, while increasing your willingness and determination to accomplish what you really want to do. Eventually, as you continue working at it you can remove all self-imposed losing limitations, and never be stuck by them again. Just be sure to monitor yourself to stay on track and keep going. You'll then be on your way to a more rewarding, meaningful life.

Change Your Habits…Change Your Life

Are some of your habits slowing you down or deterring you from making the progress you'd like to make? We're all creatures of habit; and whether winning or losing, we form habits that help shape our future.

Therefore, to win, continually eliminate any losing habits and, through constant-spaced daily repetition, form new winning habits. As mentioned earlier, it takes about 21 days to change a habit—that's all! Through consistent effort and dedication for this period of time, you can make the change. If you find yourself falling back into an old losing habit, start the 21-day period over again.

No doubt many of your habits have been with you for a long time, so changing them will require persistence. It will take the conviction that you honestly want new results enough to put forth the effort to change, being dedicated to doing what it takes for the duration of the change process.

Some of your habits could be getting in the way and actually slowing down or obstructing the realization of your dream or goal. Identify the habits you need to change so you can accelerate your progress. Take time now to think quietly and seriously, and then write them down.

Here are some examples of habits you may need to change:

- Allowing unimportant details to get in the way of priorities.
- Wasting time watching TV.
- Not taking time each day for personal development.
- Lack of organization in your daily activities.
- Lack of flexible planning.

Do any of these losing habits apply to you? Perhaps one or more of these, and others that you may be guilty of, need to be identified, listed, and changed as quickly as possible. Attack first those habits that are obstructing your progress the most. The sooner you start the better off you'll be.

Appreciate and Embrace Change

A great truism in life is that, "There's opportunity in change." Think of the enormous changes that have taken place in the world in the last 5, 10, 25, 50, and 100 years. If no one had recognized and boldly stepped up to take advantage of the changes that created virtually unlimited opportunities, where would we all be today?

Where would we be without electricity, phones, computers, the Internet, e-mail, texting, automobiles, jet aircraft, advanced medical technology, and most of the luxuries that many of us expect and enjoy every day without even thinking about it? What if no one bothered to invent, manufacture, and share these and countless other things that make our lives easier?

Use Your Imagination

Imagination is another factor that opens the door to a world of wonderful opportunities to grow and succeed. Use your ability to think and create, tapping into the powerful force of imagination. Whatever you can think of and believe you can do, you can make it a reality. As Albert Einstein discovered...

> *"Logic will get you from A to B. Imagination will take you everywhere...it's the preview of life's coming attractions."*

Because of your busy and sometimes uncertain schedule you may not be taking time to pause and think about how things are really going and how they could be. So make an appointment with yourself at least once a week, better yet once a day, and then focus on imagining what you want and what you're going to do to achieve it. This could be the most inspiring, empowering, and enjoyable time of your entire day. It'll give you a greater sense of control over your progress and help keep you on track toward your dreams and goals.

When you invest time to plant seeds in your mind and allow the creative juices to flow, your imagination will soar. You'll open doors to exciting possibilities that can lead to creative opportunities for you, your family, and growing your business or profession.

Then you may want to sit down and dream of what your brighter future could be by holding an open-minded brainstorming session with your leader or mentor, or someone else who cares about and supports you. This will enable you to discover new ways of thinking about the challenge of making it happen, while developing creative solutions as well as a plan of action.

How Can YOU Serve Others?

Take full advantage of opportunities to serve others with your winning attitude and leadership in presenting what you have to offer. Most everyone can provide something that could benefit others. Some examples could include:

1. A caring mentor or leader guiding someone in developing their action plan.
2. A compassionate businessperson offering someone an opportunity to develop themselves, get ahead, and create a better life for themselves and their family.

3. An independent business owner sharing excellent products and services that can enhance a prospect's or customer's health and appearance.

Your Rewards Relate to What and How Much You Render

The rewards you earn — emotional, material, financial, and otherwise — will be in proportion to the type, amount, and quality of the products or services you provide. A fine service or product properly marketed will bring a higher price and greater satisfaction than a lesser product or service.

Being truly supportive, sincere, and providing prompt thorough service and assistance helps you create confidence and repeat business. You'll also have the satisfaction knowing that you've done your very best to help others with what you're sharing. If you want more income help more people get what they want.

The Freedom to Create the Life You Want by Helping Others

One of the privileges you have today is the freedom to follow your dream. Among others, you have the freedom to work toward creating the life you want ... either as an employee, an independent business owner, or both.

As former US President Dwight D. Eisenhower knew full well:

"Freedom...is, in simple terms, an opportunity...to develop self-discipline."

It's only natural for a group of people to look at the same opportunity for growth and success from different viewpoints; some from a winning perspective, others from a losing perspective. Then there are those who would do well by embracing the opportunity they have right now. It's only a decision away.

So what does it mean to you to have the freedom to develop the self-discipline necessary to create the life you want...with the opportunity you have at hand? Be sure to recognize, appreciate, and take full advantage of it. Take charge and make it happen!

For example, when you see someone you'd like to introduce yourself to, be ready to seize that often-fleeting moment you have to meet them and start a conversation. You could reach out and say something relevant like ... sincerely complimenting them, commenting on the weather, or something else appropriate ... in an energetic, uplifting way. Take the lead, but relax and have fun with it!

Unfortunately, surveys indicate that a vast majority of people tend to look at where they are as being as far as they'll ever go, not recognizing their potential, settling for a not-so-happy status quo. Anyone who chooses not to change and grow has limited their potential to where they are right now! No wonder so many are emotionally dead before they even reach 30, only to live the rest of their lives with their dreams forever locked inside, their song unsung.

Since at least 70 percent of workers don't like their job, if they would build a business outside of it they could get ahead and create a life more to their liking...perhaps moving beyond the job. Imagine what that could do for their well-being and that of their families!

Just as my business was for me, the one with which you may be associated, or are considering, could be your chance to finally get ahead. Great companies and organizations always appreciate good people like you who are serious about their future and will work to contribute to and benefit from the growth and prosperity. They're expanding globally, helping countless people with their products, services, and opportunity.

Whatever their economic situation, those who are flexible and positive about creating a better future may, as I did, need to juggle priorities and make some sacrifices to move toward their dreams and goals. We all need to put forth the necessary effort to make our business or career work for us and our family. After all, nothing works all by itself. People make things work!

Making the Most of Technology Requires Interpersonal Skills

Regardless of how great a product, service, or opportunity may be, leaders and aspiring leaders who sincerely want to advance by building their business to new levels will lose if they fail to remember that, first and foremost, their business is a people business.

While technology offers convenient tools for enhancing the running of a business, it cannot make you successful! People are your most important resource, including ... prospects, customers, clients, associates, and anyone else you communicate or deal with. There's simply no substitute for building solid, pleasant, mutually beneficial relationships and giving personalized service. Always treat people with kindness in working and communicating with them.

No matter what communication method you may use always be considerate of the other person's feelings. Make it a habit to ask yourself five key questions before sharing...whether in person or via phoning, emailing, or texting...your message or information:

1. Is it necessary?
2. Is it true?

There are only two times you need to keep going: (1) When you feel like it, and ... (2) When you don't!

In line with that, there are also three kinds of people:

(1) *Those who take charge and make it happen.*
(2) *Those who sit back and watch it happen, and...*
(3) *Those who scratch their head and wonder what happened.*

Consider how frustrated you are about some aspects of your life situation and get excited about changing them. Couple this with your dream...and you'll be driven to take action!

—7—

How Resolved Are You to Succeed?

"You will succeed if you persevere; and you will find a joy in overcoming obstacles. Remember, no effort that we make to attain something beautiful is ever lost." —Helen Keller

HOW WELL DO YOU KEEP PROMISES? Talk is cheap and doesn't guarantee anything will get done. But taking winning action is priceless, and the only way to make things happen. To their detriment, many people make promises to others, or even themselves, with no commitment, which leads to disappointment, broken relationships, failure, and plummeting credibility.

Such people fail to use their time and talent to really go for their goals and dreams, leading lives that aren't as meaningful as they'd like. They know something's missing, but haven't identified exactly what it is. Unfortunately, this is extremely common. Know anyone in a situation like that?

Broken promises and the discontent that results can lead to ill feelings among friends, family, and associates. If promises are broken, it may also lead to others having a losing attitude about us and our intentions. There's no excuse for this behavior. When we say we're going to do something, we need to do it. Make sense?

Deciding Is Where and How You Begin

There are two ways to get to the top of an oak tree. You can sit on an acorn for years and wait for the tree to grow, or you can start climbing one that's already grown…right now! Don't wait until it's convenient (Success isn't built on convenience!), and don't make any excuses. Deciding is the first step toward the incremental realization of your dreams and goals. Then start doing whatever it takes to make it happen and keep going, gaining momentum.

Many people haven't taken the lead in even their own lives. They more or less live in a reaction mode, doing what they believe others expect them to do and following orders. They're often in a non-thinking robotic state, depending on the wants and whims of others. This isn't a crime but it certainly doesn't lead to success and happiness from a life of contribution...that's for sure.

No one else will make your dreams and goals come true; it's just not going to happen. That's your responsibility! The only people who may be available to help or support you are your leader or mentor, and spouse if you're married. But even if you have supportive loving family and friends, you're still in charge when it comes to your dreams and goals. It's up to you to make that quality decision about what may have been in your heart for a long time. No one else can make that decision for you. They're responsible only for their own dreams and goals, not yours.

How Committed and Dedicated Are You?

There are many definitions for "commitment." The most significant in reference to improving the quality of your life is — "a promise or a pledge to yourself to do something." Then once you've made a quality decision, commit yourself completely to making it happen. Dedicate yourself to getting the job done and achieving your dream or goal. Your dedication and effort prove your devotion after you've made the decision to do it. As former college and pro football coach Vince Lombardi offered...

> *"The quality of a person's life is in direct proportion to their commitment to excellence, regardless of their chosen field."*

Here's one of my favorite stories about dedication: A man and his wife were playing golf during a hot, humid afternoon. On the tenth fairway she stepped in a gopher hole and broke her leg. Since it was late and no one was available to assist them, he carried her and both sets of clubs back to the clubhouse to obtain medical care.

Can you picture this slight 5'6", 150-pound man carrying his 5'7", 130-pound wife and their two golf bags? Everyone was astounded and asked how he could have carried her so far. "What a feat!" they said. His response was, "It really wasn't all that bad. The hardest part was putting her down and picking her up again after each shot on the last eight holes." Now that's dedication!

But his dedication was, of course, to the wrong thing. He would have done best to stop playing golf and lovingly attend to his wife's needs. So just be sure you're dedicated to the right thing!

While understanding the importance of being fiscally responsible and generating a strong income, fine leaders put people first. They're committed to accomplishing their objectives by helping others with honor and integrity, rewarding them not only financially but also with a good feeling inside and a life of greater meaning.

Persist, Persist, and Persist Some More!

Those who make a firm decision, are committed and dedicated to it, and persevere ... no matter the obstacles ... are the only ones who can win. When challenged, they regroup and keep on going.

Be dogged in the pursuit of your dreams and goals. If you won't, who will? If you don't pursue them now, then when will you? If your job income barely pays the bills and can't possibly enable you to make your dreams come true, then take charge and press on with the opportunity at hand!

As former US President Calvin Coolidge experienced...

> *"Nothing in the world can take the place of persistence. Talent will not; nothing is more common than unsuccessful people with talent. Genius will not; unrewarded genius is almost a proverb. Education will not; the world is full of educated derelicts. Persistence and determination alone are omnipotent. The slogan 'PRESS ON' has solved and always will solve the problems of the human race."*

So emulate the achievers. Do whatever it takes, however many times it takes, to make what you want a reality.

Is Your Conviction Strong Enough to Keep Sharing and Caring?

Conviction is essential for achieving your objectives. You believe strongly in what you're doing, convinced it's the right thing to do, regardless of what anyone else may think, say, or do to discourage you. Conviction empowers you to complete the tasks associated with achieving your dreams and goals, especially when something is challenging or mundane. Is your conviction strong enough to sustain you through the disappointment of not achieving a goal at the planned-for time, as you keep resetting it... plowing ahead until the time when you can enjoy the satisfaction of actually achieving it?

Your knowledge, experience, and environment influence the strength of your conviction. To gain knowledge, always be learning to increase your people skills and business proficiency. To gain experience, go out and do what needs to be done. To improve your environment, associate with winning-attitude people. Upgrading your knowledge, experience, and environment will bolster your conviction and self-confidence.

There Are Those Who Help and Those Who Need Help!

From time to time we all need help. Since you're engaged in helping others, it's essential to share and care with conviction...

- Where there's disappointment and frustration ... share empathy and hope for a brighter future.
- Where there's a need or want...share a solution.
- Where there's a desire to get ahead...share an opportunity to earn additional income.
- Where there's a dream...share a way to make it come true.

How much you care about others is demonstrated by constantly bettering your best, while reaching out and sharing the above.

- How convinced are you that what you have to offer is beneficial and that everybody needs to know about it.
- How strong is your conviction in sharing that what you have to offer is the best solution to the challenges of your customers, prospects, and associates?
- Do you sincerely believe you can help them improve the quality of their lives through your products, services, and opportunity?
- How excited are you about sharing the hope that anyone can get ahead and live a better life, and make a difference in others' lives as well?

When you truly believe in what you're doing, tell everyone you meet about it. If you are doubtful or uncertain, then reexamine your beliefs. Is your conviction strong enough to empower you? Will it help carry you to the finish line of each of your dreams and goals?

Success isn't achieved by pushing something onto someone that they don't want or need, or think they can't afford. It's about sharing what you have to offer that could help them in some way.

Many of us share our lives in marriage. We share understanding and ideals with our children. We share friendship and loyalty with others. We share knowledge, abilities, and efforts in our business or profession. We share values and a winning attitude with everyone we come in contact with. We share compassion and ideas to help others live happier, more productive and meaningful lives.

Where would we be if entrepreneurs and business owners had not dedicated themselves to sharing their ideas, products, services, or opportunities with others? What if they hadn't kept going? Obviously, some ridicule or put down new inventions and innovative ways of doing business. But where would we be today if nobody had any conviction and would only say, "It can't be done"?

Fortunately, there are only two times you need to keep going:

1. When you feel like it, and…
2. When you don't!

In line with that, there are three kinds of people:

1. Those who take charge and make it happen.
2. Those who sit back and watch it happen, and…
3. Those who scratch their head and wonder what happened.

To get on that glorious path of taking charge and making it happen, first decide to do so! Consider how frustrated you are about some aspects of your life situation and get excited about changing them. Couple this with your dream … and it will drive you to take action!

Decision, conviction, dedication, commitment, and persistence are the key factors that differentiate excellence from mediocrity. Adopt these winning characteristics in all areas of your life and you can achieve whatever you truly desire. It's a choice you can easily make…and then implement as you learn and grow.

Or would you rather live with the pain of regret caused by not doing what you said you'd do, never knowing what you could have accomplished had you done it? Where is it written that anyone has to follow the crowd and accept an average life of mediocrity, rather than grow as a leader and create a life of excellence?

So what can you do? Take charge and make it happen for yourself and those you care about by persistently sharing what you have to offer as you grow as a leader and help others by building your business or profession.

Start It!

"When there's something to do...Start it! Don't just look at a thing...Start it!

"Don't imagine that it's too difficult...Start it! Don't put it off... Start it!

"Don't look for someone else to do it...Start it! Don't pretend you must think it over...Start it!

"Don't start half-heartedly; put everything you can muster into it... Start it!"

—Sir Walter Raleigh

—8—

How Are You Making Each Day Count for More?

"Life isn't easy for any of us, but what of it? We must have perseverance and above all confidence in ourselves. We must believe that we're gifted for something and that this thing, at whatever costs, must be attained." —Madame Curie

BE PRODUCTIVE, NOT JUST BUSY! To continue your development as a leader, use your time wisely, proactively, and more effectively…every day!

I recall a situation that caused corporate's regional vice-president to step in and confront me. First, I had scheduled a vacation during the first two weeks of November, and was also selected to represent our company at an industry-wide training council meeting in Washington, D.C., during the fourth week in November. Secondly, our agency was in contention for a company leadership award based on our year-end results. It was to be presented at the company's International Convention early the next year.

Learning of my out-of-the-office commitments scheduled for that November, he surprised me by saying, "Barnes, don't you realize you'll be out of the office for three weeks next month? I suggest you change your plans so the office can continue being productive during this vital part of the year."

After thinking about it a few seconds, I responded, "I can appreciate your concern for my office; however, if I felt that my absence would adversely affect our production, I would surely change my plans." I continued, "I am an effective leader, and I have a specific strategy for my staff's continued productivity while I'm away. If I felt I needed to be in the office for my staff to be productive I would be admitting that I was not an effective leader."

So what was the outcome of that discussion? He didn't force me to change my plans. That November my office had the highest production month in the history of the agency. We exceeded our goals!

Make Each Day Count for More!

Time keeps ticking away, regardless of whether you're on-track or off-track in pursuing your dreams and goals. Make more effective use of your time so you can achieve more of what you want in life. You'd be wasting time, deluding yourself, if you were to keep doing the same things with your time, while expecting different results.

Most people believe it's a lack of time that's limiting their income and keeping them from reaching their goals. But we all have 24 hours a day. The difference between whether we succeed or fail is how we use, or more accurately invest, our time. If we use our time ineffectively, we not only keep missing the mark with our goals, but it also adds considerable stress and confusion to our lives. Are those the kind of results you would want? Certainly not!

Investing your time wisely is vital to success...you're getting things done, the *right* things done not just anything. Since time is your most precious asset, invest it more effectively, otherwise it just disappears and you have little, if anything, to show for it.

The question is: "Are you better off?" If not, it's probably because you used your time ineffectively; therefore you didn't reach your goals. You were probably busy, but not very productive.

No one can "control" time! Seconds tick into minutes, hours tick into days, weeks tick into months, years tick into decades ... and then a lifetime! So more effective use of your time is most important in developing a successful business or career, as well as in creating the successful life you want to live. You create a more successful life by living every day more successfully. To reach your goals in as little time as possible, make each day count for more!

Every day consists of a series of choices, tasks, and actions. Some are important to your success, while others are not. Choose wisely, as each day's success depends on the tasks you chose to work on, or completed, in moving forward toward your objectives.

So How Can You Become More Effective?

To enhance the effective use of your personal and business time, start by reviewing yesterday's events. Begin with the moment you got up until you went to bed. Recall and picture the activities that filled your day, listing each one and the amount of time you spent on it. Include the time showering, shaving, putting on make-up, eating, dressing, traveling to and from work, what you did at work, what you did with your secondary income generator (be it a job or business), running errands, transporting the kids, family time, relaxing, and any other activities you were involved in.

After you've compiled your list from yesterday, continue doing it each day for seven days to get a better picture of all your activities and the time you spent doing them. When the seven days are up, review the lists and determine which activities are essential for the accomplishment of your goals, and which aren't, in moving on.

Could you have spent less time on unimportant things, such as watching TV or engaging in other non-productive activities, when that time could have been used profitably in moving toward your goal? How could you eliminate a few unnecessary activities or ones that can be delegated, to your family, for example? Arrange your activities so that you personally do only those things you cannot delegate and those that move you forward.

Some people fall into the habit of doing things that other people (besides a boss asking them to do something for their job) want them to do, even though doing so keeps them from pursuing their goals. Instead of being goal-achieving, these are often inappropriate people-pleasing activities. Or perhaps they're procrastinating what may be uncomfortable or they simply don't feel like doing.

What might you have done today that others wanted you to do that weren't goal-achieving, instead of doing what you needed to do to succeed? People who get goal-oriented tasks done and make things happen, say no to themselves and others … instead of agreeing to do things that would take them off-track.

For example, if they're asked to volunteer but need to focus on business activities, they politely decline and perhaps recommend someone else who could do it. Remember, being successful isn't a people-pleasing contest, and besides no one can please everyone all the time anyway. So forge ahead with your objectives. No one can live your life for you … nor is anyone else going to pay your bills and do what *you* need to be doing in pursuing your aspirations.

Getting goal-achieving things done every day not only makes you a winning user (investor) of time, but it can also move you toward your objective. You may be in the habit of doing only what you enjoy or perhaps maintenance-type activities. But these habits can seriously delay your progress. Do the things that keep you on track with your journey of success. Delay gratification in the short-term, doing everything necessary to achieve your goals, and you can earn the right to enjoy your dream long-term.

Six Tips on Daily Planning to More Effectively Use Your Time

1. **Diligently use a planner** or calendar, paper or digital, and always have it with you wherever you go.

2. **The best way to make progress** is to schedule your activities into your planner. Plan tomorrow's activities tonight. Don't wait for tomorrow morning to set your plans and schedule for the day.

3. **Plan your day tightly.** Schedule enough productive activities to keep you moving in the right direction.

4. **Make a list of people you need to call,** email, or text and schedule your outgoing communications so they can be done in one time slot. Leave winning messages for everyone with whom you weren't able to connect over the phone. Keep patiently and kindly following up with those on the list until you connect.

5. **Think about and plan productive activities** you can work on while you're waiting in line or for an appointment. Listen to educational and motivational audios while driving, getting ready for the day or for bed, exercising, and doing mundane chores. Keep a personal development book in print or on your phone, handy for any idle moments that crop up.

6. **You can gain nine 40-hour weeks a year** simply by setting your alarm one hour earlier and getting out of bed!

Using your time more effectively is necessary in order to build a successful career or business, while becoming the leader you want to be, better able to reach your goals, dreams, and objectives in all areas of life. This will give you more time to do the things you want and need to do for a happier more meaningful life for you and your family, as well as in your business or profession. No matter who may believe "It can't be done," as long as *you* believe it can, coupled with simply getting started and persisting in making continuous progress...you can do anything you set your mind to.

The following piece, illustrates why more effective use of your time is so important…

How Great a Producer Are You?

"The world cries for those who get things done; self-starters who see a task through to its end. It's not what you know, but what you get done!

"Most people don't succeed because they don't get things done. Their biggest handicap is not a lack of brains or willingness. It's a weakness in getting things done.

"They know what to do, and almost do it. They almost attain the next level. They almost become leaders. The 'almosts' are not lazy. They're often busier than the effective few, but still fail to accomplish much.

"They're held back by indecision and disorganization, dwelling on minor details. They keep going in circles, getting nowhere. They may chart a course, but don't stick to it. They need to work harder, and also smarter.

"It's producers who raise the standard of living, and earn the big share of the rewards. Producers are those who have formed the habit of getting things done, not allowing the 'almosts' get them off course." —Author Unknown

—9—

What Does Luck Have to Do with Leadership?

"I'm a great believer in luck, in as much as I find that the harder I work the more I have of it!" —Thomas Jefferson

WEBSTER'S NEW COLLEGIATE DICTIONARY aptly defines "luck" as—"that which happens to one seemingly by chance, fate, or fortune. Good luck is favorable fortune." While the definition of "lucky" is—"favored by luck; fortunate. Producing or resulting in good, by chance or unexpectedly; favorable. Lucky implies success by chance rather than as the result of merit."

No wonder many think that success is gained by chance rather than working for it, which couldn't be further from the truth! Anyone who claims their success is due to luck is probably just being humble. While that's certainly a great attribute, making a statement like that does a great disservice to those who want to be successful … and would love to learn how. Humility could more appropriately be expressed by thanking those who led, mentored, and encouraged them and, as appropriate, otherwise recognize those others who contributed, depending on the situation or environment.

I've been told that I've been lucky in my business and personal life, because from all outward appearances it looks like good fortune has smiled on me and my family. Yes, overall, we've enjoyed good health…a winning attitude has a great impact on this … and, thankfully, an abundance of happiness and prosperity. However, I've discovered that truly successful leaders' so-called luck could be more accurately described using the following acronym:

- **L** is for Leadership
- **U** is for Understanding and Upgrading
- **C** is for Capabilities and Communication
- **K** is for Knowledge

Since we can and do...in reality...make our own luck, let's examine these four ingredients:

1. Leadership

Leaders have a vision, a purpose, and a mission to guide them, coupled with an appropriate sense of urgency...and they know the difference between efficiency and effectiveness and employ both. Efficiency is achieved by doing things right, while effectiveness is achieved by doing the right things.

Leaders are proactive, not reactive; they take charge and make things happen. They don't follow the average-thinking crowd; they follow their dream or objective. Leaders lead by their winning attitude, behavior, and actions, not just by what they say. They walk their talk, leading others by example, inspiring and empowering them to do and accomplish things they otherwise couldn't or wouldn't.

2a. Understanding

Leaders point the way for others to follow, not from obedience but from understanding. They listen with empathy because they have an understanding of human nature and have experienced similar challenges on their way to becoming leaders. My mentor taught me early on that people knowledge—an understanding of and skill with people—is paramount for achieving success.

Since everyone has certain fundamental desires, a basic understanding of the following will help you appreciate why people think, feel, and act as they do:

- **Desire for belonging.** Everyone wants to feel as if they're needed and wanted by certain others. This was most evident when you were a teenager, if you "followed the crowd" as many teenagers do. As you've matured, however, you have a better sense of who you are and what *you* want and need to do, realizing that "the crowd" isn't doing all that well. Since you want to be more successful, you've developed the desire for belonging with a group of winning-attitude people.

- **Desire for friendship**. Most people have lots of friendly acquaintances; but true friends, not so many. True friends not only care about each other through challenges with empathy, encouragement, and perhaps guidance, they also enrich each other's lives, sharing hopes, dreams, triumphs, and joys.

  However, to maximize success and happiness in business we can benefit by taking friendship to a new level ..."productive friendship." We're steadfast and supportive of each other, while taking mutually beneficial actions in working together to achieve goals and objectives in a way that reflects each other's needs, wants, dreams, purpose, and aspirations.

  As businesspeople sincerely build productive friendships they bond in a common cause, growing and becoming what they were created to be, improving their own lives, as well as that of others, helping make the world a better place.

- **Desire for ownership and assets**. You work hard and smart and use your money wisely, while generating income and accumulating assets to build an estate for you and your family's financial security and well-being. You're grateful for all that you own, no matter how little you may have.

- **Desire for accomplishment.** Whenever you reach a goal that's important to you or make a dream come true, that makes you feel good ... increasing your self-esteem, self-confidence, happiness, and joy.

- **Desire to know we make a difference.** We all want to feel that we matter, and be recognized and appreciated for the winning attitude and abilities that enabled us to do something that made a difference. While it may appear to be unimportant to some, what you did is important to you.

  Being recognized is a powerful force to motivate people to bigger and better accomplishments; and as we grow and expand our outreach, we start realizing that we can make a larger difference in the world. Anyone who doesn't receive appropriate appreciation or recognition for positive results may simply quit on themselves and others ... who could otherwise benefit from what they have to offer.

- **Desire to live the dream.** Ever since you were a child you've undoubtedly dreamed about being, doing, and having certain things. Humankind has advanced so spectacularly, especially over the last century, because of people who have dared to dream of and do what seemed impossible. Your dream motivates you to take certain actions every day toward making it a reality. You may want your kids to have the funds for college. You may dream of...a new home, baby, vehicle, happy marriage, working from home, financial independence, travel, more time with family, and enjoying more of your interests and hobbies, as well as having a carefree retirement.

- **Desire for gain.** You want to get ahead so you can live a better life...being, doing, and having what you truly want for yourself and your family...elevating your life experience.

- **Desire for security.** You want to accelerate your income to fulfill these two basic desires, both strong motivators to excel in your career or business. You work toward a secure future for yourself and your family, planning and acting specifically to achieve that.

  As you grow and develop, you realize more and more that your security is in your ability to produce. In developing a track record of achievement, you're more likely to feel more self-assured to set ever bigger, more exciting goals.

2b. Upgrading

Why do so many allow their desires to be trashed or forsaken? Average tendencies, to whatever degree, if not understood, overcome, and upgraded to winning tendencies, keep people from realizing their desires. Leaders have already dealt with those proclivities and therefore can help their people do the same.

For anyone still challenged by any average-thinking tendencies as described below, be heartened. Begin right where you are, continue going and growing...and you can accomplish what you desire.

- **Average-thinking people tend to procrastinate.** Although they may not admit it, they have a tendency to put tasks and decisions off. They often need to be encouraged to make winning decisions, set priorities, and to take action now... otherwise they'll stay stuck or regress.

- **Average-thinking people tend to sabotage their own success.** They make losing decisions, choosing the so-called easy way out. Fortunately, many who are now followers can become leaders...provided they're empowered to grow! They must not allow themselves to be influenced by average-thinking people who aren't moving on and don't want anyone else to either. Misery loves company! They would benefit by associating with winning-thinking people who are moving on.

- **Average-thinking people tend to give up when confronted with a challenge.** They probably don't realize that overcoming challenges is fundamental to creating a better life, and doing so yields tremendous satisfaction! Some challenges, like rejection, are just normal experiences when anyone is in the process of getting ahead.

  No one should ever take rejection as a personal affront, as if something's wrong with them or what they're offering. They need to know they can handle whatever comes their way as they reach out to others with what they have to offer. Guide and encourage them to grow, do whatever it takes to get and stay excited, and embrace challenges with a winning attitude, while consistently taking action toward overcoming them … so they can achieve their desires.

- **Average-thinking people are often broke, lacking the willpower to save money.** They shy away from making the sacrifices needed to do so, the lack of self-discipline being a deterrent to saving. If they're experiencing this challenge, they need direction and encouragement to overcome it.

  Financial difficulties are common … especially with today's buy-now-pay-later mentality. It takes money to live, but to provide well for tomorrow requires delaying gratification and working toward generating more income today.

  Encourage these people to commit themselves to earning and saving enough to become financially secure, and then work toward accumulating sufficient wealth to achieve the financial independence they want. This requires dedication and perseverance in supplementing their income, while saving money, or they'll never be able to get out of debt and make their dreams come true.

- **Average-thinking people tend to worry about the future.** They worry about job security, their financial situation, their children's futures, their health, and just about anything else imaginable. Their average thinking and focus contributes to creating exactly what they're worried about. They tend to be anxious to find an easy "quick fix" type solution that will relieve them of their worries and anxieties.

  An excellent way to help such people is to direct them to view things differently … in a winning way rather than an average way. This can assist them in reducing and eventually eliminating their concern about the future, while replacing their average thinking with winning expectations. Worry won't improve any outcome, nor increase anyone's lifespan. It only depletes energy that could be put to much better use by taking action to get ahead!

Now that you have an upgraded understanding of these basic human desires and tendencies, you know what drives or holds people back. This enables you to respond and take action in leading yourself and others in a winning supportive way.

As you continue growing, you can rise above any average-thinking tendencies you may still have and become stronger in those areas. This helps you accelerate on your journey of success, while avoiding the detours that those tendencies may have caused you to take in the past. You can then better understand and upgrade your own mind-set, and encourage others to do the same. It'll be easier to have a winning attitude about all the situations you experience, while observing what others are going through. Then, with your upgraded level of understanding, you can also lead them to a more meaningful rewarding life for themselves and those around them.

3a. Capabilities

People develop their capabilities through education, environment, observation, and experience. Top achievers learn far more from being in "the school of actually doing it" than from any formal education they may have received. They develop greater capabilities by focusing their attention on consistently acquiring education and experience in their arena, enabling themselves to excel, lead, and get ahead. They also associate with others who are moving on, which encourages them, changing worry into faith, hope, and action.

Successful people are just ordinary people who do extraordinary things ... diligently applying themselves to the task at hand. They realize that continuous learning and fine-tuning is imperative for ongoing progress toward any worthwhile goal. Are you always learning, developing your capabilities, and honing your skills? It's up to you to make those choices so you can better serve your family and those who could benefit from what you have to offer.

3b. Communication

Leaders communicate by behavior and actions...their example... not just by what they say. To communicate effectively, remember that it's 93 percent non-verbal while the words you say account for only seven percent. Your body language, tone of voice, and what you actually do communicates most of your interest, sincerity, intentions, and feelings. Be sure that your body language is appropriately reflecting the messages you want others to receive.

Leaders listen—a vital aspect of leadership! They open their minds and hearts in caring about others' wants, needs, dreams, and goals. Since we can't talk and listen at the same time, and we think faster than anyone can talk, listening requires true sincerity in focusing on what the other person's saying. Listen to gain clarity and understanding so you can determine the action needed to best serve your associates, customers, and prospects … as appropriate … when mentoring, or sharing an opportunity, product, service, or even when giving a referral.

In this modernized version of what he said, George Washington summed it up well…

> *"When someone speaks, be attentive and don't interrupt. If they hesitate in what they're saying, don't help them unless they ask for it, nor respond until they've finished speaking."*

4. Knowledge

Knowledge, the final ingredient in "LUCK," is key to growing as a leader. Unfortunately, once most people graduate high school, trade school, or college they stop learning anything beyond what's required for the job. But those who want to grow as leaders realize a diploma, certificate, or degree is just the beginning of what needs to become life-long learning. They diligently develop themselves personally and professionally, while advocating it for those they're mentoring or leading.

Leaders thirst for knowledge, which is a result of a winning attitude, commitment, perseverance, firm dedication, and a super tenacity in working toward their dream, goal, or objective. Knowledge is essential for growing in leadership and achieving the results that enable us to live the life we want. The acronym LUCK could also mean Labor Under Correct Knowledge!

Every now and then someone would ask: "Why are people like you so lucky when most aren't?" To me the answer was clear: "Nobody lucks into being successful. I found that the harder and smarter I worked the 'luckier' I got!" "Luck" could also be defined as — "when opportunity and preparedness meet." Your greatest opportunities can be found when you meet new people and you're prepared to help them. This is where a purposeful meaningful life of getting ahead, while making a difference, can be found!

The secret to an enthusiastic winning attitude is to constantly focus on, anticipate, and work toward your dream or objective.

You're excited by what you're doing and where you're going, eager to reach new levels. You're adventurous and want to live life to the fullest, embracing it with a renewed sense of wonder.

Be enthusiastic in everything you do, at home, on the job and in business. This attitude, alone, yields its own opportunities ... like attracting other enthusiastic people and those who'd like to be. Who wants to be around energy-draining negative people?

Enthusiasm is a tonic that energizes everyone to be more confident and productive, enabling them to be kinder, happier and more likeable.

What if more people were like this? Imagine the great leaders who'd emerge and what a difference they'd make!

—10—
How Does Enthusiasm Affect Leadership?

"Enthusiasm is the yeast that makes your hopes shine to the stars. It's the irresistible surge of will and energy to execute your ideas."
—Henry Ford

ENTHUSIASM MAKES A HUGE DIFFERENCE! It's that certain something that enables you to be a leader and do great things. It pulls you out of the mediocre, commonplace, humdrum, lackluster mentality of being average...and releases your energy. It makes you glow and shine, lighting up your face.

ENTHUSIASM—the emotion that makes you "sing" and attracts others to "sing" with you.

ENTHUSIASM—it's a maker of friends and smiles, and a producer of hope, happiness, and motivation. It shouts to the world, "I've got what it takes to lead and I'm making it happen." It tells everyone that your career is great and your business is the greatest, and the goods, services, or opportunity you're offering are the best.

ENTHUSIASM—the inspiration that makes you wake up and live more fully. It puts a spring in your step, a song in your heart, a twinkle in your eyes; and it gives you confidence in yourself and others to get things done.

ENTHUSIASM—it changes a person with a deadpan personality into one who produces, a pessimistic-thinker into an optimistic one, a person who loafs into a go-getter, a follower into a leader.

ENTHUSIASM—when you have it be thankful for it. If you don't have it, do whatever it takes to develop it!

Enthusiasm Is One of a Leader's Greatest Assets

Are you waiting for someone to come along and say, "Wow, have I got a fantastic life for you!"? Or are you fired up with enthusiasm for leading yourself and others to creating a better life? With enthusiasm, even everyday tasks are readily handled. People with enthusiasm like to get going and keep going; they like to lead!

In your private life you'll reap tremendous benefits because of your enthusiasm. You'll even approach the things you do for fun with a new sparkle and zest. Your friends and family will become much more than just the same old faces you might otherwise numbly stare and scowl at after a challenging day at work. With enthusiasm you can even do those basic household chores with a winning attitude. An enthusiastic attitude enables you to enjoy life more.

So What's the Secret to an Enthusiastic Winning Attitude?

What healthy food is to energy, enthusiasm is to a richer more meaningful life! How can you unlock its benefits? There's no magic formula or password. It simply starts with your attitude. The secret is to constantly focus on, anticipate, and work toward your dream or objective. You're excited by what you're doing and where you're going, eager to reach new levels. You're adventurous and want to live life to the fullest, embracing it with a renewed sense of wonder.

Be enthusiastic in everything you do, at home, on the job, and in business. This attitude alone yields its own opportunities ... like attracting other enthusiastic people and those who'd like to be. Who wants to be around energy-draining negative people? The bliss you experience from being enthusiastic is beyond compare, a priceless quality no money can buy. It lights up your life and uplifts those around you.

So fire up your enthusiasm and carry it with you always, sharing it through your caring, other-centered, winning attitude. It'll permeate and positively influence every fiber of your being. Your health will benefit, and you'll realize more joy, satisfaction, and meaning in all areas of life.

Enthusiasm is a tonic that energizes everyone to be more confident and productive, enabling them to be kinder, happier, and more likeable. What if more people were like this? Imagine the tremendous leaders who would emerge and what a difference they'd make!

You may feel enthusiastic inside, yet reticent to show it, afraid to let your real self shine for fear of being criticized. If so, simply start using words that convey enthusiasm like...wonderful, terrific, excellent, outstanding, tremendous, and sensational that can get you, and those around you, excited! This enlivens your communications and helps make you a winning-attitude "people magnet."

Some confuse enthusiasm with impatience. But impatience is a losing attitude that can cause a fanatical, greedy drive to success, often leading to errors in judgment and using others. Enthusiasm, however, helps us accomplish things in an upbeat friendly caring way, especially when leading and sharing with others.

Enthusiasm and Leadership Are Founded on Self-Esteem

As more discussion on this was promised earlier, self-esteem is the respect we feel for ourselves, reflected in how well we perceive our own worth and potential, as well as the level of belief we have for reaching it. Self-esteem is key to being enthusiastic, and governs leadership and success in all areas of life. You can be enthusiastic only to the degree that you have self-esteem, which is essential for achieving your dream or objective, as well as in supporting others in doing likewise. Fortunately, self-esteem can be enhanced!

Our thoughts, feelings, and dreams get reinforced, ignored, or negated as we grow from childhood to young adulthood ... and beyond. While most youngsters have boundless dreams, how they're treated by their parents, teachers, family, friends, peers, and others either builds up or tears down their self-esteem. Developed over time, self-esteem is affected by the beliefs we have about ourselves, as formed by our thinking, perceptions, experiences, relationships, roles, job, social status, age, health, and media influences.

Ultimately, however, it's our *own* thoughts that most influence our self-esteem; and we can choose new winning thoughts to increase it. Our past does not determine our future...unless we let it! If you've never questioned the validity of any losing ideas you were led to believe about yourself, such as someone putting you and your dream down, you've lived your life as if that were all true, severely limiting your potential.

Your actions, behaviors, and feelings are consistent with and reflective of your self-esteem. When it's healthy you feel a sense of well-being, secure in your aspirations and free to express enthusiasm for them. If you don't have self-esteem you feel unworthy and insecure about your aspirations, unable to express enthusiasm for them...and likely to have a just-getting-by life!

For many, particularly those who aren't growing and developing themselves, or have fallen back into losing thinking, their self-esteem wanes. This is especially true when they fall prey to those who tease, criticize, bully, or devalue them or what they're doing. Some try to hide their lack of self-esteem by being arrogant, constantly joking, showing off to look successful when they're not, and avoiding criticism by making excuses for not taking charge…acting as if they have all it all together. But this won't help them advance.

Raising Self-Esteem So You Can Pursue & Achieve Aspirations

Self-esteem blossoms when we regularly associate with other upbeat success-oriented people who care about, affirm, and support us in our quest, as we're growing and developing, going forward with a greater sense of meaning and purpose. Since getting ahead in life depends on growing self-esteem, it's important to have at least one person with high self-esteem, perhaps a mentor or leader, who believes in and encourages us that we can do it.

All of this helps keep our spirits up and feeling good about ourselves. The habit of hiding behind any facades falls away as we increase our belief in ourselves and our potential in doing what we've chosen to do, demonstrating authentically who we are.

Some people will like us and what we're doing; others may not. No matter how much we may want everyone's approval, it's just not going to happen, nor does it matter! We all have our own life to live; and while naysayers are entitled to their opinion, we are not held hostage by them! This attitude is quite liberating, allowing us to freely embrace and pursue the achievement of our ambitions.

Enhancing your self-esteem enhances your life; and no person or circumstance can prevent you from doing so when you want to strongly enough. The degree to which you enhance it is proportional to the degree to which you believe in your potential, without falling back into any losing attitudes you may have had about yourself.

Evict any limiting ideas that may have been dwelling in your mind, and move on from their hold! For example: lack of self-confidence and people skills, being unassertive and indecisive, choosing to remain a follower rather than growing as a leader, lack of focus and organization, difficulty accepting compliments, believing you need a diploma or a degree when it's not required, believing you can never earn others' respect, being vulnerable to negative opinions, making excuses instead of pressing on, fear of failure or even success, or, in general, lacking self-esteem but doing nothing to enhance it.

Don't allow naysayers' opinions, un-affirming thoughts, or limitations steal into your mind like thieves in the night. They'll only rob you of the great treasure of self-esteem. They're only false prophets or beliefs … traitors to your growth as a leader that need to be recognized and guarded against at all cost.

Leaders reject falsehoods and break through limits, whether self-imposed or pronounced by others. As all leaders have, you, too, can enhance your self-esteem and be a bigger winner! Like anything worthwhile, it takes time depending on where your self-esteem is at the moment. If you want to be a more positive, enthusiastic person, strive daily to think and act only in a winning, enthusiastic manner.

Enhance your self-esteem by thinking only winning thoughts about yourself. Answer a key question…"What kind of a person do I really want to be?" If doubts or losing thoughts creep into your mind, evict them! Be resolute. Picture only what you want, and strengthen your commitment to making it happen. Believe you're capable of growing and becoming more of who you want to be.

Never accept being down on yourself. Instead, write out and daily affirm something like, "I believe in myself, I have a lot to offer the world, and I do whatever it takes to accomplish my goals. And since I'm a winner in the game of life, I'm up or I'm getting up!"

If you've ever taken a golf or tennis lesson you've probably had a similar experience. During the first few days following the lesson, you may not play very well. As you continue, however, to practice, practice, practice in a positive, focused manner, you gradually become better and better at it. At the end of a two-or-three-week period you probably will have learned the necessary changes to your approach and your game is likely to have improved.

Likewise, this kind of disciplined regimen will enable you to upgrade your self-esteem and the attitude, skills, and habits associated with being a leader. You'll grow more enthusiastic … feeling it physically, mentally, and emotionally; and it becomes contagious, causing others around you to catch it! Your increased self-esteem, the foundation of your enthusiasm and success, will go a long way in making your journey to your dreams and objectives…void of any self-imposed restrictions or roadblocks.

You'll get better at stopping yourself from putting barriers in your way, and eventually overcome the habit of sabotaging your own success. Rather than focusing on why you can't do something, you'll focus on how you *can*, not letting anything get in your way of taking charge, growing as a leader, and making it happen.

Finally, ask yourself…"Do I feel enough respect for myself to grow as a leader and do whatever it takes to give myself and my family the life we want?" Developing your self-esteem is absolutely essential for you to ignite your enthusiasm for success and make your dreams come true, while leading others in doing the same!

Dealing with and overcoming challenging situations strengthens your optimism, builds confidence, and develops self-esteem.

As you courageously meet and overcome circumstances, you clear the path to your dreams, goals, and objectives, enabling you to achieve the results you're striving for.

Excellent leaders put forth more effort, perform better, and accomplish more than everyone else, understanding adversity is the companion that spurs them on, helping them grow.

They rise above their circumstances, refusing to use them as excuses for not achieving their goals, refusing to be a victim of anyone or anything.

—11—

Leaders Leverage with Circumstances to Succeed

"Until you've dedicated yourself to some worthy cause, purpose, or endeavor you'll never overcome your circumstances and become the leader you're ultimately capable of being."

—The Publisher

LEADERS USE CIRCUMSTANCES to propel themselves in overcoming the challenges they encounter in reaching for their aspirations, and help others do likewise.

Without a dream or objective, there's no reason to do anything out of the ordinary. It's the single biggest *why* you can have that will drive you to grow and become the person you were created to be, so you can accomplish what's in you to do. The bigger your dream, the more goals you set. The more you accomplish based on a worthy purpose, the more happiness and meaning you find in life.

Leaders are dreamers who attract others like a magnet. People love to be around them and their winning energy. Dreaming is contagious. When you help others realize they can do something to improve their lives...whether via a product, service, or opportunity ...and empower them to do so, your business or career can soar!

Remember, "success" is — "the incremental realization of a worthwhile dream or objective; it's not just an endpoint." It's built on the three cornerstones of...

1. Goal setting.
2. Action planning.
3. Doing whatever is necessary to make it happen.

When joined together they form the strong foundation on which all success is built!

Now let's put this definition under the light. Let's say you have a worthy dream, maybe several. If so, decide which one of them you want to experience first. Maybe it's the one you've had the longest, perhaps even since you were a kid. Choose the one you're most passionate about achieving.

Goal setting is attaching an achievement date to that dream. When do you want to make it happen? What steps do you need to take to do so? For example, if you want to move to a new level in your organization, what needs to be done to accomplish that? Attach dates to each stepping stone along the way. If necessary, ask you leader or mentor to review your goals and give you guidance.

Next, taking the required appropriate action is the only thing that can result in the realization of those dreams and goals ... provided you stick with it and reset those goals, as necessary, until you reach them. Goal setting and taking action are as inseparable to success as night following day, yet they're equally distinctive. They're two sides of the same coin. One side asks "Why and When?" while the other asks "What and How?" Together they can lead to success.

"Someday" Becomes a New Word Called "Never"!

Having a cherished dream or objective without setting intermediate goals and doing the required follow-through activity is merely daydreaming. "Someday" is simply a fantasy that becomes a new word called "never."

Make your goals feasible by being actively engaged in a career or business that can provide you with a viable way of working toward their attainment. A plan of action is needed, but creating one loosely described, without goals, is a waste of time and energy.

When you set worthy goals and weld them to a plan of action, diligently take that action so you can propel yourself to success.

It's really quite simple. So why, then, don't most people succeed? They fail to follow through! For the same amount of time and energy as they use doing miscellaneous things that don't lead to their dream, they could have gotten closer to realizing it. As humorist Will Rogers quipped...

> *"Even if you're on the right track, you'll get run over if you just sit there."*

Just when you're about to reach a short-term goal, immediately set a new one, then continue moving onward and upward. The only way to coast is downhill, which won't get you anywhere but the bottom! Since time's slipping away you're losing ground if you're not advancing toward realizing a heartfelt dream. That's why leaders work smarter as they progress through life.

The more successful you want to become, the smarter, and more diligently and effectively you'll want to work toward your aspirations. If you're in a people-helping-people field like I was, your results also depend on the size of your customer or client base and how many associates you lead in working smarter and being more productive as well.

When average-thinking people reach a short-term goal they tend to back off, rest on their laurels and lose momentum, which only sabotages their success. They need to re-ignite the passion they originally had for their long-term goal...their dream...and use it to motivate themselves.

Have you ever noticed how winning-attitude people keep having success after success and, conversely, how average-thinking people don't? Success is the result of setting goals based on achieving our dream or objective, developing and following a plan of action, and working through challenges to completion, while effectively leading ourselves and others. Otherwise, our objectives fade into oblivion, "failure city," as "someday" becomes a new word called "never"!

The choice is ours. We either take charge and make it happen...or we don't! Once you've identified the dream or objective you're most passionate about, set an achievement goal date, develop a plan with short-term goals...and take action!

A Guide for Leadership by Dreams, Goals, and Objectives

Have you established your motivation—your dream or objective? Have you set goals to achieve it?

- **What motivates you?** What's your greatest desire, dream, or objective? What do you *really* want to accomplish for yourself and your family? You may consider others' suggestions, but only you can identify what you strongly, sincerely desire. Don't let circumstances or what others think, say, or do dissuade you from going for what you really want. You can do anything you set your mind to.

- **What income do you need to live a better life?** What leadership level are you striving for? Incorporate those objectives into your goals. What if you had only a year to live? Wouldn't that give you a sense of urgency? Give your goals that urgency now. Time's marching on!

- **Write out your goals and target dates,** and periodically evaluate your progress related to the timetable you've set. Adjust as necessary until you make it happen. It may help to do this with your mentor or leader at agreed upon intervals.
- **Don't let your current capabilities** or accomplishments hold you back. When your desire's strong enough, you can overcome whatever obstacles you meet along the way.
- **What tools, products, and services are available** to help you achieve your goals? How can you best take advantage of e-commerce and other resources in utilizing your company's or organization's website? Always be looking for opportunities to grow yourself and your business or career.
- **If you want a new home,** what type, price, and area would be appealing? Dreambuild by going to open houses.
- **If you want more financially security,** start supplementing your income and saving more...so you can accumulate the amount you'd like to have available by a certain date.
- **Your business or career goals may need to** include a specific number of presentations per day, week, month, or year, depending on your objective.
- **Share your dream only with supportive people,** like a leader or mentor, to whom you can be accountable. If you're the only one who knows what you're aiming for, no one else can encourage you. While having someone to be accountable to can help, it's most important that you hold *yourself* accountable, resetting your goals until you reach them!
- **Start fresh when you're setting, and striving toward,** your goals. The past is over; it's time to move on. Believe wholeheartedly that you can accomplish whatever you've decided to achieve. How strong is your work ethic? What changes, if any, in your work ethic will help you reach your goals? Are you going to approach previously untried prospects? Will you commit to doing more than you've ever done before?
- **Will you work harder and smarter to accelerate** the realization of your goals? Will you use your life situation as an excuse not to or a reason to be motivated in striving for your goals? Might you need encouragement or guidance from your mentor or leader? Do whatever it takes if you honestly want to succeed and be happier.

What Drives Achievers to Keep on Keeping on?

Achievers diligently invest the time and energy required in goal-achieving activities, reading personal development books, and associating with winners. But what drives them to continue going above and beyond achieving their initial dreams, goals, and objectives?

- Receiving a tremendous sense of satisfaction as they lead and mentor others in pursuing their dreams, goals, and objectives, and seeing them accomplish such.
- Being appreciated for making a difference, while remaining humble. They know their success is due, in part, to the guidance and encouragement *they* received from a leader or mentor who they readily acknowledge. They know success isn't a solitary venture, and their humility reflects that.
- Establishing a foundation and being a philanthropist.

Your confidence in all areas of your life can soar when you're persistently pursuing your aspirations while helping others in various ways. It'll put a spring in your step, a smile on your face, and excitement in your eyes!

Your Future Reflects What You're Doing to Create It

If you haven't already done so, start being the leader in your personal life, family role, and career or business...setting goals, focusing on your dreams, and encouraging others to do the same. Unlike those who are drifting through life, not totally understanding why they are where they are and how they could change the situation, growing as a leader enables you to better your future.

Here are two important questions to ask yourself...

- "What business am I in?" The people-helping-people business, right? All businesses are to help people in some way!
- "What's my mission, purpose, objective, or dream?" What's driving you to do what you're doing?

If something's worth doing it's worth doing well. Go for it, and when you make a mistake learn all you can from the experience. It's part of the process. Success comes in the doing. You can better set your priorities and goals by asking yourself the following questions...

- Is your mission, purpose, objective, or dream well defined?
- Why do you believe you're here on this earth?
- What value can you add by doing what you feel good about?

- How would you invest time to grow yourself?
- How would you go about doing whatever it takes to build your income to where you really want it to be?

You set goals to begin your journey, but to set your plan into motion and achieve them you need to work. Plan your work then work your plan, as covered in chapters four and eight.

While setting goals, you'll be influenced by both your personal and business life. Although it's important that you set goals to satisfy your personal wants and needs, you also need to consider how they will fit into the overall goals of your family. In addition to that, what do they want and how can you support them in getting it?

The direction your goals take is directly related to the impact of your particular desires. What do you really, really want to achieve? What have you been pushing aside? Will you make the necessary sacrifices? Will you do whatever it takes, day by day, to make it happen and not let circumstances get in the way? Are you going to grow beyond your situation or let it stop you?

Another advantage of leadership by dreams, goals, and objectives is that you have something to focus on and move toward, and you can control and measure your performance based on your incremental results. This will help you more powerfully motivate yourself to continually strive toward your desire because it's always in view.

Imagine you're being beckoned to come and claim your dream. Think of it as being on layaway. As you continue paying toward it, serving more people and reaching your goals, whatever that requires, your dream will eventually be paid-in-full, becoming a part of your new reality. You'll own it free and clear, and then have the opportunity to dream even bigger dreams and work toward making *them* a reality. Your life is one exciting adventure after another!

Self-Discipline Is Key to Leadership

Self-discipline is founded on and driven by desire, the lifeblood of all success. Leaders demonstrate it as they passionately pursue their dream or objective...while inspiring and encouraging others to do so as well. They don't allow themselves to be influenced or pushed around by negative thinkers or circumstances that would interfere with what they want to accomplish.

Have you ever heard expressions like, "Everything they touch turns to gold"? Or "If they fell into a pile of manure they'd come out smiling and smelling like a rose"? Those with a grand dream or objective, strong desire, a can-do attitude, and a well-thought-out plan of action coupled with follow through…will succeed provided they desire it strongly enough to keep them going until they get it.

Once you've committed to pursuing your dream or objective, you start growing as a leader by first leading yourself…persevering in doing whatever it takes, including, for example:

- Working harder and smarter, while putting in longer hours.
- Continuing your education by reading positive books, listening to motivational/educational audios, viewing webinars, and attending seminars to upgrade your knowledge and skills.
- Seeing the positive side of an event even though it may appear only as a negative. Always look for the good.
- Being thankful for challenging experiences. There is no such thing as failure—it's a learning experience along the way to your goal. You discover what works and what doesn't.
- Being a good follower in emulating your leader, but not being content to remain one. Grow as a leader and set the pace!
- Setting a good example while you're growing as a leader, showing others how it's done. Don't expect anyone to do what you aren't willing to do. Walk your talk!
- Developing your self-esteem and self-confidence so you can more effectively care about and best lead others.
- Teaching your people how to build their dream … inspiring and encouraging them to do what it takes to realize it.
- Matching and exceeding the efforts of the leaders in your industry. Take the lead and become a superstar.

Look at these things as adventures in taking action in growing as a leader. Help those with average mentalities who want to grow, turn things around and rise above their challenges. Caring about them as you persevere with a winning attitude can help give them the boost they need to make it happen. Remember, how and what we think forms the foundation of our success or failure. Negative thoughts cause negative results; positive thoughts cause positive results. The course of our lives is determined by our thinking!

Those who believe in themselves can reach any goal they set, as long as they're disciplined to do whatever it takes to achieve it. Belief can give you the mindset to do wonderful things in your life…even improve it a lot…when you really, really want to. Self-belief can lead to creating the success you want, provided you don't do things that don't support or justify that belief. Unsuccessful people think and say one thing, but do another. Don't be one of them! Be congruently and proactively positive in all your thoughts, words, and actions.

For example, some may think or even say they're go-getters when they're actually wasting time watching TV instead of pursuing their goals. Until they shift their thinking to eliminate the contradictory behavior, they'll forever be stuck. It would do them good to identify some leaders in their industry to admire, ask for their guidance and encouragement, and then emulate their self-discipline and other success attitudes and behaviors.

What Does It Really Mean to Be "Self-Made"?

We've all heard of, read about, or may know successful men and women who are considered self-made. But how did they rise up from being underdogs? Why do they stand out from the crowd?

The truth is we're all self-made! While the successful self-made are looked up to, the average ones aren't. The successful did whatever it took to make themselves successful, while the others typically followed the crowd that just isn't doing all that well, making themselves average. Either way, successful or average, both are self-made.

To become a self-made success requires the cooperation of other people through leadership. It relates to what someone makes of themselves based not on financial or any other advantages, but mainly on their attitude, desire, focus, work ethic, personal growth, people skills, and professional knowledge, skills, actions, and accomplishments.

The self-made successes who inspire us most did inspiring things while overcoming great obstacles. Their successes can then be used as examples to empower and lead still others to take charge, make it happen, and become self-made successes themselves.

Why Do Some Say that They're "Under the Circumstances…"?

The idiom "Under the Circumstances" is defined as—"because of the difficult nature of the situation" … often citing a lack of time, money, or something else, without giving it a second thought. Unfortunately, many people use the circumstances they're in as though they were victims being held "hostage" or having to do something against their will. They readily give in to them as if they were unalterable directives from a nasty superior, or they could be fearful of someone or something. Have you ever noticed that?

So, then, why are some people so successful, while others not so much? Successful people work around and blast through circumstances no matter how challenging, regarding this as part of their growth process. Learning all they can from them, they turn circumstances into winning situations, using them to spur themselves toward the success they want. Your attitude and beliefs determine whether circumstances will either stop or motivate you. The choice is yours. So, why not use circumstances to drive you forward?

Many people say they don't like their circumstances, yet they're unwilling to improve their attitude and do something to change the situation. Therefore, they remain ineffective and find themselves constantly struggling, never getting ahead.

But if you come across someone who complains about being "under the circumstances" who would sincerely like to improve their situation, as a growing leader you could empathize, ask what they want, offer a solution, and then encourage them to go for it!

Have you ever thought about why some people in similar circumstances and environments succeed while others fail? Those who succeed keep their eyes on their goal as they take charge and make it happen…regardless of whatever circumstances they're in.

As Martha Washington exclaimed…

> *"I'm determined to be cheerful and happy in whatever situation I may find myself ... the greater part of our misery or unhappiness is determined not by our circumstances but by our disposition."*

Can You Change Your Circumstances?

Is it possible to be positive and productive enough to change the circumstances of your life? YES! What do leaders do? They discipline themselves to conquer their obstacles. They become stronger and more empathetic through overcoming adversity and are better able to lead others to help them achieve their goals. Whenever they encounter a challenging circumstance they learn from it, grow through it, and keep moving! As someone wise offered…

> *"There are times in everyone's life when something constructive is born out of adversity…when things seem so bad that you've got to grab your fate by the shoulders and shake it."*

We all encounter many circumstances in life; some more easily dealt with, while others may require a lot more work. How well you handle them will largely dictate your progress in achieving your aspirations. Your inclination and readiness to deal with these circumstances promptly and effectively will be apparent from your outcomes. While some may be expected and some seemingly come out of nowhere, most will be the result of your own choices.

The good news is, as you courageously meet and conquer circumstances you'll be clearing the path to your dreams, goals, and objectives…and further enabling yourself to more effectively confront still more circumstances that arise in the quest for ever greater achievements. All of this strengthens your optimism, builds self-confidence, develops self-esteem, and supports your ability to create the circumstances you want!

As George Bernard Shaw observed…

> *"People are always blaming their circumstances for what they themselves are. I don't believe in circumstances. The people who get on in this world are the people who get up and look for the circumstances they want, and if they can't find them, make them."*

Fine leaders focus their energy, work intelligently, build productive friendships, and accomplish more than most, leveraging with adversity as a companion that spurs them on. They rise above unwanted circumstances and create favorable ones, never using them as excuses for not pressing on toward their goals. They refuse to be victims of anyone or anything else.

There's another benefit to disciplining yourself in pushing ahead, conquering the obstacles threatening to hinder your progress. As you overcome them you become more invested in what you're doing, causing you to value your goal even more while growing stronger in leadership and achievement. Remember, where there's no investment there's no value!

As you do whatever is needed in hurdling challenges, it becomes more exciting as you gain momentum, realizing you're getting closer to a dream, goal, or objective. You know in your heart that there's *no way* you're ever going to quit! You persevere until you get it done, and then keep going, accomplishing more of what you want to accomplish.

A self-motivated person determines what they really want, sets goals, develops a plan of action, and undauntedly puts that plan into motion. They not only benefit themselves in doing so, but also their family, business or career associates and any other stakeholders who are positively affected by their leadership. Everyone wins!

Develop your people skills, the ability to understand, interact, and work effectively with others, seeing them as they can be, not just as they are.

A leader's success is affected by his or her people skills, backed up by product, service, and opportunity knowledge. For example… communicate clearly so you're understood, and listen to understand what they're relating back to you.

If your people fail to follow your recommendations, unless they're obstinate, you haven't reached them. Have you addressed their concerns?

Your results will tell you how effective you are!

—12—

How Could You Enhance Your Ability to Lead?

"The growth and development of people is the highest calling of leadership." —Harvey S. Firestone

ARE YOU A LEADER OR A MANAGER? While they have some things in common, there are others that differentiate them. As you may recall, the main difference is that managers control things and activities, while leaders empower people!

A "leader" is defined as—"one who leads; a guide; a conductor; a chief commander." By their actions, a leader sets the example for others to follow, inspiring and encouraging them to do things they otherwise wouldn't or couldn't do without the leader's influence.

Much of this chapter is based on my career leading an insurance agency from absolute bottom to second from the top ... nationwide! The concepts and ideals are pertinent and valuable regardless of the business or profession you're in. They're also useful in dealing with the personal aspects of your everyday life. Understanding the art of leadership is fundamental to becoming an effective leader.

The single most important thing in building a strong, dynamic organization is the leader's attitude, which, of course, needs to be a winning one. This, coupled with compassion, understanding, and dedication toward followers makes for a winning combination. Believe strongly in what you're doing and don't let anyone buy into any pity parties. While others may commiserate with your people, it's incumbent upon you to lead them out of their quagmire...so they can move onward and upward to success.

Whatever you do, always exhibit leadership qualities. For example, a working mom often has many responsibilities … family, job, and perhaps a business she may run from home. She also makes time for appropriate social and other activities, which may even include running a business with her husband.

As a leader, a business owner often engages in a myriad of activities, such as … sharing or "selling," presenting, mentoring, teaching, inspiring, encouraging, empowering, prospecting, building relationships, and other human relations activities.

Ten Keys to More Effective Leadership

In growing as a leader you want to maximize the results of your efforts, so here are ten principles for performance and effectiveness:

1. **Think of yourself becoming a more effective leader.** Be enthusiastic and, above all, optimistic. Look for the good in people and situations, and how best to get things done.

2. **Develop bifocal vision.** Focus on two of the most important aspects of your career or business: people and productivity.

3. **Set priorities.** Do the most important things first, investing your time and energy where it counts most for achieving goals and objectives.

4. **Build on two success factors:** respect for the company or organization, and confidence in your leaders.

5. **Teach new associates your business's system of success,** what they need to know and do in order to succeed. Help them focus on goals and dreams, their reasons to excel, teaching and leading them by your superb example. Don't assume they know anything about the business or organization you're in. Start from the beginning with the basics of a proven system that people can understand and apply to incrementally realize their objectives.

6. **Lead by positive expectation.** As a role model, give your associates something great to live up to.

7. **Edify your leaders/mentors.** Openly express admiration and respect to and for them and what they've done for you and your business or career. This affirms them and supports their credibility, making it more likely that your people will heed their guidance and emulate their fine qualities.

8. **Lead with solid commitment.** If you're not committed, your associates won't be either. Encourage them to have a high level of commitment. Establish an excellent relationship with them, and build a friendship and a "success-ship" with them. Teach them how to set goals and reach them.

9. **Teach people how to focus on what they want**. For example, encourage them to test drive their dream vehicle, take pictures of their dream home and post it where they can see it, get travel brochures, watch inspiring movies related to what they want, and imagine how they would feel living their better life. Teach them to stretch and grow toward their potential by your example in doing so.

10. **Acknowledge your associates and their successes,** such as mastering new skills and reaching new levels, showing you care about them and what they've accomplished. Since 95 percent of people underestimate themselves and what they can do, this helps build your associates' self-esteem and self-confidence. Encourage and assure them that they can achieve their objectives going forward.

Where you've been or where you are isn't important. It's where you're headed that really counts. Demonstrate the following qualities in your mentoring and training, but keep it simple. Be consistent, predictable, and dependable, and use the power of repetition. If they don't get it at first, repeat your teaching until they do.

A Business Success System Is Vital

The system mentioned in #5 of the above list refers to a proven pattern of success as developed for your particular business. This means choosing to follow the plan, method, or approach recommended and taught by the leaders and reinforced by the suggested educational/motivational materials and such. When chosen to be followed, methodical techniques and general procedures can maximize everyone's potential for success. If you're new or unsure of how to proceed, get the specifics from your leader or mentor.

Never assume everyone understands, embraces, and is applying the basics of the system. Associates need to be taught the unique specifics and the importance of applying them. But even if they're doing so, they could get distracted and go off track, making repetition essential for them to embrace their leader's attitudes toward the system, that is, if they honestly want to succeed in the business.

As a growing leader, you also need to know and apply the basics so well that your associates can emulate you and effectively teach and show others. This saves you from "micro-leading," doing it all yourself, to spawning capable leaders down the line who then do what you're doing in leading others. As I did, you're growing your business or profession as a working participative leader, demonstrating teamwork and what to do by actually doing it, instilling competency and confidence in others who will also run with it.

But if someone tries to lead by personality, alone, they'll never be an effective leader. Having established procedures in place will enable your people to grow and become the best they can be. Leaders bring out the best in others by caring about and encouraging them, while giving the best of themselves.

Personal Development Is Essential for Getting Ahead a Living a Better Life ... Even More So for Leadership!

Personal development is essential for everyone who, first and foremost, wants to get ahead and live a better life. And it's even more essential for those who want to grow in leadership and advance to greater levels of success, while encouraging associates to do the same. You can lead people only to level you've reached, both in personal development and achievement!

Choosing to take advantage of the personal development tools and opportunities that may be offered by your business or profession, as well as learning its leadership philosophies and principles, helps keep you going and growing. Key to your success and that of those you're leading, this could include: availing yourself of inspiring and empowering books, audios, courses, trainings, seminars, webinars, conventions, and other resources and activities ... as may be recommended by your company, organization, or leader. For example, you could read a personal development book 15-30 minutes a day, and listen to a success audio daily.

While no one can personally develop anyone else, choosing to attend business-related functions will provide you and your associates with more knowledge while stirring enthusiasm, and may also serve as a forum for recognizing new levels of achievement. Associating with others who are moving on helps build everyone's confidence in themselves as well as in your business or profession, builds esprit de corps, and rekindles eagerness.

Set an example for others to follow; people are more inclined to emulate your actions rather than do just what you say. Back up your words with action. Show your people that you're taking advantage of personal development tools and learning opportunities, and they'll be more inclined to do the same. Growing leaders take initiative and set the pace. As Ralph Waldo Emerson exclaimed…

> *"The pace of the pack is determined by the speed of the leader!"*

How Proactive Are You in Making Decisions?

Decision making, or the lack of it (which is also a decision!), is one of the most serious concerns in business and life today. People frequently hesitate or won't make a decision that they'll be held responsible for. They're often afraid they'll make a mistake, fail, or perhaps even be rejected by their peers who aren't moving on.

For example, while someone with high hopes may sign up for an opportunity to supplement their income, when they encounter their first challenge they fail to take charge and apply themselves to growing through it and making it happen. As George W. Cecil shared…

> *"On the Plains of Hesitation bleach the bones of countless millions who, at the Dawn of Victory, sat down to wait and in waiting…they died. [Don't be one of them!]"*

The decision-making process presents an opportunity to be a leader, a champion. People can choose to either become effective leaders of themselves, as well as others, or perhaps stay stuck and languish in the mediocrity of the so-so, same old same old. But regardless of their initial strengths and weaknesses, becoming a leader depends mostly on the drive and determination to grow into it.

When a decision needs to be made, gather the facts and consider the alternatives. While making a decision is important, it's imperative to know the following as you proceed:

- What and who will the decision affect and when?
- What question or circumstance is the decision based on?
- Have both sides been given the chance to air their views?
- Is the decision an appropriate response to the question or circumstance?
- Does the decision provide a win-win solution?

While making effective decisions always be open-minded, consider the options and, if necessary, seek guidance from those more knowledgeable and experienced.

In your desire to make a decision to start something new or to solve a pressing challenge, first stop worrying about it. That only saps your energy. Do your best to make a quality decision, then strive to make it work for everyone concerned.

Continued worry won't change a thing. It normally just keeps a person stuck in the "paralysis of analysis." But once worry is put aside, the decision is made to get the wheels of progress rolling, and appropriate action is taken, the results will start revealing themselves. From then on, give it your best...no matter what the results may turn out to be. Take responsibility, adjust things as necessary, and keep moving.

As you go through the decision-making process, select and focus on the most significant task within it and you might be amazed at how well and quickly you could realize the desired outcome depending on how things develop. When it's completed, you can go on to other priorities with a clear and open mind. You will have become more effective because you methodically made the decision, giving yourself the freedom to implement it ... and then you can move on to the next important thing. You're leading yourself!

More Key Skills for Effective Leadership

A leader can easily master knowledge by studying, learning, and doing. But skills are developed only by actually doing them, getting better and better as you go. Experience, sometimes referred to as "the school of hard knocks," is invaluable as you grow and move forward through the vicissitudes of business and life. You do something new and often get immediate feedback, either through your own gut feeling or via the response of others.

Here are five more skills for you to increase your capabilities in growing as a leader:

1. **Know what to do and how to do it** ... so you can lead by example. To increase the potential of your people in making more and better presentations, do so yourself so they can watch and emulate you. The same is true no matter who you're leading or what you recommend that they do.

2. **Develop your people skills**, the ability to understand, interact, and work effectively with others, seeing them as they can be, not just as they are. A leader's success is affected by his or her people skills, backed up by product, service, and opportunity knowledge. For example...communicate clearly

so you're understood, and listen to understand what they're relating back to you.

If your people fail to follow your recommendations, unless they're obstinate, you haven't reached them. Have you addressed their concerns? Your results will tell you how effective you are!

3. **Be solution oriented.** Again, problem-solving skills and decision-making skills are essential for effective leadership.

4. **Be humble and teachable at all times.** In order for us to be successful, we all need others to do their part. To think otherwise is foolish. Unhealthy pride, egotism, or arrogance, never serves anyone. They have no place in relationships and, in fact, destroy them.

5. **Continuous personal and professional development is essential for growing as a leader**. The finest leaders are always learning and growing. Anyone who stops learning and growing stays stuck or regresses. Stay fresh. Keep learning and growing.

Taking action grows your confidence, which has no substitute when you're leading people. This, of course, is provided you don't take yourself too seriously and mentally beat yourself up while you're going through the learning process. As you develop competence, you can teach and instill confidence in the people you're leading. You've done and are doing what you're teaching and showing them to do. As long as you stay humble in the process, you can grow and shine as a leader.

Thinking and Planning

Since thinking and planning are vital for growing as an effective leader, be sure to make time for this activity every day. Helpful ideas will usually come to you after some careful, committed thought and consideration on your part. When that happens, let go of your conscious thoughts and allow your subconscious mind to take over. You could also sleep on an idea or challenge, and you might be amazed at how it all starts coming together the next day.

For example, Thomas Edison, renowned inventor, would consciously think about and research ideas, then take a short nap to, relax his conscious mind. Upon awakening, his subconscious mind would take over, and wonderful new ideas would pop into his head.

As Norman Cousins observed…

"We… have everything we need except the most important thing of all—time to think and the habit of thought…the basic energy in human history. Civilization is put together not by machines but by thought."

Great insights can occur when you're relaxed or not consciously thinking about the situation in question. The solution to a challenge or a useful new idea will hit you seemingly like a bolt out of the blue. But these ideas don't come out of nowhere. You've already given it a wealth of conscious thought, research, focus, and concern beforehand, raising your awareness and openness to a solution.

The point is, however, after you do this research and thinking, but still aren't coming up with what you need, it's time to let it go for a while. Stop thinking about it, and go do something else. You've prepared your mind, opening it to the ideas or solutions that will appear later with no further conscious thought.

Louis Pasteur put it like this…

"Chance favors only the prepared mind."

Don't waste time and energy worrying about things you can't control. Instead, change your attitude to one of acceptance, not letting any situation paralyze you from doing what you need or want to do. On the facetious side, if you believe you must worry, schedule a time to just worry! For instance, you could worry every Sunday afternoon from 2-to-3 pm. Worry about this or that, but when 3 p.m. comes and the alarm goes off, don't worry until next week at the same time! This allows you to have 167 hours of worry-free time every week!

Remember that worry won't extend your life one second, and it won't change any outcomes. You'll just waste a lot of time and energy getting yourself all worked up; time and energy that you could better use to pursue your dream or do something else of value.

A great alternative to worrying would be to use the worrying hour to think and plan the actions you're going to take. When the appointed time comes, put all else aside. After informing others who might interrupt that you're not available, close the door and turn off your phone. Sit back, relax, and focus on your dreams and goals and what you're going do to work toward achieving them during the coming week, putting the activities into your schedule.

Amazing, productive, and beneficial thoughts will flow from your subconscious mind, empowering you to build your business or profession. The great side effects of this quiet thinking time are that you'll feel wonderful, excited, positive, and worthwhile. This experience may sound trite, but it works.

Leadership—More Food for Thought

Here are five additional facts about leadership that deserve to be mentioned:

1. **Set priorities and do those things that need to be done** to reach your goals and dreams or at least to continue your progression toward them. Follow your plan.

2. **Knowing what to do is certainly important, but follow-up action is also essential.** Behavior is visible, knowledge is not. For example, knowing how to build your business or profession but not doing it doesn't serve you or anyone else.

3. **Learn to truly listen; nothing new can be learned while talking.** Listen not only to what people say, but also listen beyond their words to what they don't say, which is often the real message. Listen with empathy as this opens your heart to them. Maybe all they need right now is for you to just quietly listen. Everyone needs to know someone cares.

4. **See yourself as you really are.** You may not always like what you see but it probably represents at least some truth about yourself. Be honest. Write down all your positive qualities, then list any traits that you'd like to change.

5. **To change, first know** what you're changing from, your starting point. Then envision yourself as you want to be.

6. **As a leader and business owner** you get paid for the results you achieve by inspiring and empowering others in your organization who achieve profitable results.

Without Truly Listening There Can Be No Real Understanding

As mentioned, listening is an integral part of effective communication. But listening and truly hearing and understanding what others are saying are not the same. We can listen without understanding, but we can't really understand without truly listening and, as necessary, asking relevant questions to get clarification.

Empathic listening includes paying close attention to what is being said. Always listen with an open, uncluttered mind. Don't be thinking of what you want to say in response until they've stopped talking. Quiet your mind and focus on the person talking and hear and understand what they're saying. If you allow yourself to think of other things while pretending to listen, the talker gets the feeling that you don't really care. The only way for them to feel understood is for you to be quiet and focused on listening to them. Good conversation is a dialogue, not a duel of monologues.

Once again, remember this: People don't care how much you know until they know how much you care. Leadership is built more on this idea than practically anything else. People are more likely to follow those who truly listen to them. Listening shows you care. Few people do it well and you'll stand out as a leader.

Observe and Mentor

An effective leader is a good observer and mentor. One approach that can work wonders is to periodically meet with those you're leading. Review what's been happening and what their goals are for tomorrow, next week, next month, and next year. Such a review can be effective in helping people stay on track and moving in the direction they need to go to reach their goals.

Here are some other items you could cover:

1. **Recognizing what they're doing well** which is usually reflected in their results. However, even though someone's making good presentations, they may still be encountering a string of noes. Encourage them to maintain a winning attitude, keep meeting and befriending new people, and fine-tuning everything as they go.

2. **Where they need to improve** their attitude, knowledge, personal development, presentation, and people skills.

3. **What they need to be doing** if they want to make more progress...every day, week, month, and year.

4. **What else they can do to produce better results.** For example, appropriate grooming, appearance, and clothing may need to be adjusted for more relatability and acceptance.

How Are Your Relationship-Building Skills?

Skills in relationship building are central to your growth as a leader. The relationships you build with your people are more consequential than any talent you may have. You could have all the talent in the world, but if you don't build excellent relationships you'll have no one to share it with or assist. Talent is the capacity for top-notch performance in a specific area.

With a caring, growth-supporting, cooperative relationship of mutual respect with others, along with a positive attitude, your people's performance can improve dramatically... whether or not they're particularly talented. They can make up for it with courage, determination, a teachable attitude, and extra effort. With those qualities, they could outshine your most talented people who aren't as motivated! Talents and other qualities, when multiplied by your relationships, lead to increased productivity.

Remember that while nobody can do everything, everyone can do something. As a leader, you want to bring out the best in people. Surround yourself with self-motivated people who are making progress, succeeding. Create a positive environment and be there to encourage them as they, too, navigate the "bumps" and "potholes" encountered along the way.

Participative Leaders Get the Best Results

There are at least two distinct styles of leadership—autocratic and participative.

- **Autocratic leaders** have a dictatorial attitude that says they, alone, have the power and are in control. They make all decisions by themselves and for themselves, even if they don't realize it. Such leaders operate through manipulation and intimidation, instilling fear in their people. It's an archaic way of leading that destroys rather than creates any potential for positive relationships.

  Such leaders want "yes people" around them who won't disagree. This style of leadership builds resentment and hostility, and motivates people to move away from them in order to escape their tyranny...if they have the courage to do so.

- **Participative leaders** believe in the potential of their people and encourage them in developing it. They're humble, express their heartfelt feelings, and have a personal caring philosophy toward and a positive expectancy of their people. They offer honest compliments, encouragement, and support. They help their people identify what they want or need, and empower them to go for it. They set the example of how to be and what to do by actually living it and doing it themselves, thereby inspiring others to be that way as well and do what needs to be done…so everyone can accomplish their objectives.

Inspiring and Empowering People to Excel, Not Power and Control, Is the Responsibility of a Leader

Some personalities need more participation and guidance from their leader, while others are more confident self-starters who can do more on their own with less oversight and assistance. Effective leaders are flexible and adapt to the needs of their people.

The primary objective of a leader is to maximize the productivity of their people…so they can all reach or exceed their individual goals. This then enables leaders to reach or exceed their own goals. A leader's responsibility is not to have command over people, but to contribute to the success of an organization and its people. Function, not power, is the business of a leader.

As the sage advice based on a Chinese proverb reminds us…

> *"Give someone a fish and he or she will eat for a day. Teach someone to fish and he or she will eat for a lifetime."*

The best leaders care about and mentor individuals … considering their needs and aspirations within the context of the opportunity the particular business or organization provides. People have different personal histories, experiences, ages, education or training, ethnicity, races, socio-economic positions, values, ideals, personalities, beliefs, situations, goals, dreams, and objectives; and it's these differences that contribute to making leadership such an exciting, challenging adventure. Your ability to recognize, respect, and leverage with those differences helps you lead others on their journey in incrementally realizing their aspirations, and can result in tremendous success all the way around.

Who Am I?

"I am your constant companion; your greatest helper or heaviest burden. I'll push you onward or drag you down to failure. I am completely at your command.

"Half the things you do, you might just as well turn them over to me, and I'll be able to do them quickly and correctly. I am easily managed; just be firm with me.

"Show me exactly how you want something done, and after a few lessons I'll do it automatically. I am the servant of all great people… and of all failures as well.

"Those who are great, I have made great. Those who are failures, I have made failures. I am not a machine, but I work with all the precision of a machine and the intelligence of a human being.

"You may run me for profit or ruin; it's the same to me. Take me, train me, be firm with me and I'll put the world at your feet. Be easy with me and I'll destroy you.

"I am the Law of Cause and Effect on autopilot. Who am I? I am HABIT!" —Author Unknown

—13—

How Does the Law of Cause and Effect Relate to Successful Leadership?

"It's dangerous to refuse to continue learning and knowing more...Don't give up because the pain is intense right now—get on with it, and before long you'll find that you have a new vision, a new purpose." —Oswald Chambers

AS WE ALL KNOW, ACTIONS HAVE CONSEQUENCES; for every effect, or result, there's a cause, a reason why. It's the Law of Cause and Effect. Our attitudes, thoughts, beliefs, behaviors, habits, and actions produce the effects that shape our career or business, and the life we live. We reap what we sow!

The Law of Cause and Effect vitally impacts successful leadership, which is no mere happenstance. It's caused by various winning ingredients such as: an uplifting can-do faith-filled attitude; a fervent desire for the dream or objective; belief in self and committed to the mission; great people skills; cares about others; being available; a strong work ethic; makes no excuses; takes responsibility; high integrity; charisma; always learning, growing, and developing themselves, while mentoring and encouraging associates to do the same; and makes the most of opportunity. Yes, there are various causes for successful leadership, but the main cause is...YOU!

The Law of Cause and Effect is also vital when it comes to failed leadership, which results from various losing ingredients, such as: a boring can't-do doubt-filled attitude; lackluster desire for the dream or objective; unsure of self and the mission; poor people skills; lack of concern for others; not available; a weak work ethic; makes excuses; shirks responsibility; low integrity; lacks charisma; doesn't learn, grow, or develop themselves, while not mentoring or encouraging associates to do the same; and takes little or no advantage of opportunity. Yes, there are various causes for the lack of or failed leadership, but the main cause would be…YOU!

Your results (effects) are based on your actions or inactions, which cause the consequences you experience. You have free will and may act as you choose, but you simply can't escape the inevitable consequences of your actions or inactions. You alone are responsible for your actions and their effects, even if you did something (or not) at the suggestion, request, or demand of another.

Remember to take the time to think and plan every day. Think about what you need to do, and how and when to do it, to change the challenging circumstances you're experiencing, so you can achieve winning outcomes. Consider what effects your actions could have, not only on your goals but also on those you're assisting in reaching their goals, and those they're helping to do likewise. Strive to create results where everyone benefits. That's a mark of a leader.

Look at yourself as objectively as possible, appreciating that you're a unique individual with virtually unlimited potential for growth and success. By honestly observing the effect (result) of what you've created in your life, business, or career so far, you'll notice that the cause revolves around you … your perceptions, beliefs, attitudes, and what you did or failed to do.

You Become Like the People You Associate with and Vice-Versa

Choose your friends carefully; seek and associate with winning-thinking people who encourage you to be your best you. Emulate leaders you respect and admire in your business or profession.

When you meet someone who's struggling, see them as an overcomer and help them boost their attitude, thereby boosting your own. Then as you care about and help those who choose to buy from or associate with you, your life becomes more rewarding and meaningful!

Is Your Environment Conducive to Your Growth as a Leader?

Your environment is more influential to your growth as a leader than your heredity, so look at how you've set up your life. Is your environment contributing to or detracting from your efforts to becoming the best leader you can be? If not, you may need to modify it in order to realize your dreams and goals and those of your family. For example, if you want to build a business on the side, you may need to rearrange your home environment to better accommodate that. What else could you change about your environment to support your success in growing as a leader?

What's Beckoning You to Grow as a Leader?

Are you making the changes you need to make in order to realize your aspirations? Are you involved in personal and professional lifelong learning, while upgrading your knowledge, people skills, and motivational level? Are you being coached by those you'd like to emulate who are where you want to be?

Is your vocation or day job suited to your personality, interests, and objectives financially and otherwise? If not, change is beckoning you to lead yourself in the direction of your greatest hopes and dreams, and becoming the person you were meant to be.

In growing as a leader be sure to care about others in supporting their success and happiness…as well as your own. The more people you inspire, empower, help, and serve the more you'll grow into being the leader you want to be, enabling you to achieve more and make a bigger difference.

What Could You Do to Increase Your Income?

Since very few people will ever have significant sums of money just handed over to them without working for it, most have to earn it; and there are only two ways to do that:

1. You work for money via a job, a business…or both.
2. Money works for you via profitable investments made with excess income.

Most people earn money by working for someone else, as an independent business owner, or both, which is a popular option in today's world. Regardless, the money is received after the work is done. Those used to a regular paycheck may expect to receive an income as soon as they start a business, not realizing that it takes time and effort to build it to a certain level of productivity and profitability… *before* any income can be received.

As an employee, you work to earn the money you need to provide for you and your family, the amount of which is the effect of your job role and activity.

If you're not happy with the amount you're currently earning, rev up your enthusiasm and do something to increase your income, like building an independent business on the side, which is generally run from home. Stay focused and productive, applying what you're learning so you can reach new levels, while doing whatever is necessary to achieve this and other important objectives. Be the cause of it happening so you can enjoy the fruits of its beneficial effects.

An Exciting New Vision Will Cause Your Optimism to Soar!

Here are some more ideas to help you maintain a winning attitude, while growing as a leader who achieves greater success by helping others:

- **Upgrade your enthusiasm by focusing on** the exciting new vision you have for your life. Without it, your job, business, other activities, and marriage, no matter how exciting initially, can grow stale with time. Stay fresh and invigorated by imagining how it will feel when you start living your vision.

- **Eliminate the monotony of your routine** by being creative and flexible in putting some variety into your life. Take a new route to work, enjoy a new restaurant or hairstyle, rotate home tasks, make positive new friends, and build a business on the side. Put eagerness into every day and boost the vitality of your productivity in all areas.

- **Dream BIG and work toward creating** your better life every day. Whether your future life remains as your life is now or develops into what you'd like it to be depends on you and what you do to create it. Never give up no matter who may try to dissuade you or whatever obstacles you encounter!

- **See the "Big Picture" of your life, job, and business** relative to your objectives. You're the only one who can limit yourself, regardless of what others might think, say, or do. You have the final say in the goals you set and what you do to accomplish them. So shed the shackles of boredom and do something exciting that empowers you to go above and beyond for your greatest, most cherished dream.

- **Finally, see yourself, your career, business,** and whatever else you do, and how it all affects the most important people in your life … family, friends, associates, the community, and even beyond. Know that what you do with and in your life really matters, that you're making a positive difference, and realize you can do so even more going forward.

As you grow in leadership, keep focusing on the exciting new vision you have for your life and your organization, and do whatever it takes in causing it to unfold before you. If you don't you'll never know how great it could have been, and find yourself living with regret for having abandoned your vision. Don't go through life lamenting, "If only I would have grown as a leader…."

Since the world is suffused in negativity, think in positive winning ways for yourself, those you lead and serve, and all who could be affected by your attitude.

Realizing your exemplary leadership can be the catalyst for countless others to get ahead and live a better life helps you persist and feel good about your mission as you grow and become all you were meant to be.

Your dedication to helping others, along with your unwavering commitment to the highest principles and values, will light the way for those who now live in the frustration and unhappiness of an everyday ordinary status quo life.

You have the opportunity, as well as the responsibility, to care about, encourage, and empower others for greater growth and accomplishment...as you inspire them with your exemplary leadership to be all they were meant to be, mutually finding the true success, happiness, and meaning everyone yearns for.

—14—

So What Does It Take to Be an *Exemplary* Leader?

"Maturity begins to grow when you can sense your concern for others out-weighing your concern for yourself."

—John H. MacNaughton

DO YOU HAVE THE LEADERSHIP QUALITIES of those who serve as the best role models; those who are exemplary? Such leaders care deeply about people, and have a noble calling that guides them in leading their organization as they make a difference for countless others, leaving a legacy.

Exemplary leaders strive to be as efficient and effective as possible by working on high-priority goal-achieving tasks rather than just on tension-relieving maintenance-related tasks that can by done by others, done later, or left undone. They also strive to attract other exemplary leaders, as well as potential exemplary leaders.

Exemplary leaders point the way for others to follow, not by expecting obedience but by being understanding. They listen with empathy because they're concerned about others' well-being, having gone through challenging situations themselves and, with the help of *their* leader, grew through them. They are quite proactive, rather than mostly reactive like average-thinking people tend to be. They make things happen, often in a big way, rather than watching or wondering what happened.

Exemplary leaders exude unwavering eagerness, a winning attitude, strong commitment, and sincere dedication. They earn others' trust because of their unshakable integrity and impeccable honesty. They're gracious, humble, appreciative, and always in a learning and growing mode. Strong self-confidence, healthy self-esteem, and consistent self-discipline are also hallmarks of exemplary leaders. They back up their words with straightforward enthusiastic action! As Dr. Norman Vincent Peale so aptly stated…

> *"When you have zest and enthusiasm, you attract zest and enthusiasm. There's real magic in enthusiasm. It's the difference between mediocrity and accomplishment."*

Exemplary Leaders Create Caring Winning Environments

They want others to feel nurtured, optimistic, appreciated, and free to blossom into all they can be and find greater success, happiness, and meaning. They're sensitive, compassionate, and forgiving, exercising sound judgment in bringing out the best in people. They encourage strengthening interpersonal relationships and working synergistically, while acknowledging everyone as valuable to the team.

Exemplary Leaders Inspire and Empower Others with Charisma

Rather than telling people what to do, exemplary leaders energize them to follow their lead with charisma—the personal "magnetism" that sets them apart from the crowd. It's the balancing of qualities in a consistent personality that almost anyone can relate to, such as:

1. Confident yet humble, and readily connects with others.
2. Laughs easily and has good clean fun with people.
3. Upbeat, encouraging, inspiring, and hope-inducing.
4. Strong, yet kind, compassionate, caring, gracious, and warm.
5. Open, easy to approach, friendly, and delightful to be around.
6. Greets others with a smile; has good eye contact and handshake.
7. Puts others first and listens intently, making them feel important.
8. Honors people by repeating and remembering their names.
9. Well aware of what's going on and able to tell relevant stories.
10. Has a sparkle in their eye and a spring in their step.

You may say, "Wow! That's a lot to live up to." Fortunately, charisma can be developed, as these qualities are typically learned and acquired through environment, experience, and following the lead of others. What qualities might you need in order to create the right balance for more charisma in yourself? Start developing them today! Most people have the talent, capacity, and knowledge to perform far better than they do, including increasing their charisma.

As Thomas Edison knew firsthand…

> *"If we would do all we were capable of doing, we would astound ourselves!"*

Exemplary Leaders Encourage a Strengthening of Will!

Will—desire coupled with determination—needs to accompany skill. Is your will strong enough for you to be more and do more, so you can achieve more good in all areas of life than ever before?

Everyone can benefit by being more inspired and encouraged! Exemplary leaders provide that by taking a sincere interest in people and setting a fine example to follow, while promoting that they strengthen their dream. This is done by discovering what they need or want and helping them cultivate their will for achieving it. It's an exciting challenge as no two people have the exact same desire and determination, which contributes to making growing as an exemplary leader such a grand adventure!

So What's the Difference Between a Boss and a Leader?

The following comparison was presented during a leadership training seminar conducted by Kinder Brothers, *Patterns of Professional Management*, titled **"Be a Leader!"**

"The boss drives his or her people; the Leader coaches them.
The boss depends on authority, the Leader on goodwill.
The boss instills fear; the Leader inspires enthusiasm.
The boss says 'I'; the Leader says 'We.'

"The boss says; 'Get here on time';
The Leader gets there ahead of time.
The boss fixes blame for the breakdown;
The Leader fixes the breakdown.

"The boss knows how it's done; the Leader shows how.
The boss says, 'Go'; the Leader says, 'Let's go.'
The boss uses people; the Leader develops them.
The boss sees today; the Leader also looks at tomorrow.

"The boss commands; the Leader asks.
The boss never has enough time;
The Leader takes time for things that count.
The boss is concerned with things;
The Leader is concerned with people.

"The boss lets his or her people know where he or she stands;
The Leader lets his or her people know where they stand.
The boss works hard to produce;
The Leader works hard to help his or her people produce.
The boss takes the credit; the Leader gives it away."

Key Attributes of Exemplary Leaders

Exemplary leaders have specific attributes, some of which were touched on before, that are part of their deep-rooted philosophies and principles. Here are 25 of the best...

1. **They're possibility thinkers,** solution-oriented rather than problem-oriented.
2. **They're loyal** toward their company, organization, associates, customers, clients, and other stakeholders.
3. **They truly care about others** and always work toward mutually beneficial outcomes.
4. **They're committed to** their mission, guided by a solid value system as they pursue their objectives.
5. **They proactively make decisions,** considering the variables and, as appropriate, input from others.
6. **They treat others with respect and fairness,** appreciating them for who they are, the good they're doing, and their potential; and they live by "The Golden Rule—Do unto others as you would have them do unto you." If they fail at any of this, they take responsibility and do their best to recognize the deficiency and rectify the situation.
7. **They're even-tempered and forgiving,** and competent in their relationships. They know what they stand for, and have a good sense of where they stand with others.
8. **They humbly share the limelight.** They know they didn't get to where they are alone and readily admit it. They give credit to and appreciate any assistance, big or small, that they receive along the way.
9. **They lead by example,** while constantly upgrading and fine-tuning their knowledge, understanding, and skills.
10. **They have impeccable morality,** and earn respect by their sterling behavior.
11. **They're wholeheartedly enthusiastic** and have an unrelenting winning attitude in all they do. Their enthusiasm is contagious, and their associates almost inevitably catch it.
12. **They encourage healthy self-esteem** in their people, recognizing its direct relationship to success and happiness.

13. **They help to keep their people excited and growing** by recommending personal development books, as well as audios, functions, and other resources of value.

14. **They take responsibility for their decisions.** If a decision was incorrect, they own up to it, learn from it, and take remedial action.

15. **They share their dreams, goals, and objectives** with their leader or mentor as a way to keep themselves accountable and on track.

16. **They inspire, encourage, and train new leaders,** helping them feel they're a valuable part of the team, causing team members to feel good about themselves and their roles.

17. **They keep lines of communication open** and encourage honest feedback. They root out rumors and do their best to get to the bottom of them before they spread and create disharmony, fear, and potential chaos. They don't gossip, but instead talk about ideas rather than people.

18. **They're excellent, focused listeners.** They know they can learn nothing while they're talking.

19. **They dream constantly,** always going for bigger dreams, keeping themselves motivated. They dreambuild regularly with associates to help keep them going, and teach them to do the same for themselves and others down the line.

20. **They don't take themselves too seriously,** have a great sense of humor, and keep things fun as appropriate.

21. **They're service-oriented** in all they do in their career and business, as well as in their personal lives.

22. **They have the faith and inner strength** to face and overcome obstacles, setbacks, rejections, and failures without being diverted from their mission.

23. **They love what they do,** and focus on tasks that will get them where they want to go. They don't waste time on activities that would detract from achieving their objectives.

24. **They have a keen sense of urgency,** but never aggressively force things to happen, maintaining a patient yet moving-forward attitude. They keep on going, doing what

they need to do, knowing it's normal for challenges to arise, and that a delay is not a denial.

25. **They passionately pursue their vision** until it becomes a reality. They then pursue ever greater visions, making a bigger difference, often becoming philanthropic, inspiring others to emulate their sterling example.

Exemplary Leaders Live Their Vision, Mission, and Purpose

Your *vision* is the loftiest expression of what you actually want your life to be. It's your mental picture of hope and optimism of the ideal. You may be familiar with these powerful biblical words…

"Where there is no vision, the people perish."

A *vision* might relate to, for example, how an independent business owner would like his or her organization to be. You may have a vision for your business expanding around the world, impacting people everywhere in a positive way.

A *mission statement* reflects what and how you contribute to the world. It's based on how you are implementing your life purpose, for example, through building your own business.

Your *life purpose* relates to what you are meant to do with your life, why you're here on the earth. Purpose is at the core of both the mission and the vision, which originates in the heart and soul of a business's owner or founder.

Perhaps they've discovered certain products and services that have enhanced their health, beauty, appearance, and other areas of life. Having taken advantage of an opportunity that enables them to do so, they enjoy sharing them with others who could also benefit.

All the while, they're developing into the person they were created to be, becoming an exemplary leader as they keep getting ahead and living an even better life. They take pleasure in reaching out to others and building new friendships, making a difference in a special way…with the goal of helping more and more people.

Living on purpose will make you feel good about yourself and what you're doing. You'll be serving others the best way you possibly can in line with fine values, principles, and aspirations … which are integral to a richer, happier, more meaningful life experience.

Exemplary Leaders Are Servant-Leaders!

As Robert K. Greenleaf, founder of the modern-day servant-leadership movement, offered…

"The servant-leader is servant first... Becoming a servant-leader begins with the natural feeling that one wants to serve, to serve first. Then conscious choice brings one to aspire to lead. That person is sharply different from one who is leader first... The difference manifests itself in the care taken by the servant first to make sure that other people's highest priority needs are being served.

"The best test, and the most difficult to administer, is this: Do those served grow as persons? Do they, while being served, become healthier, wiser, freer, more autonomous, more likely themselves to become servants?"

But You May Say, "I'm Not a Leader of Any Kind!"

While that may be so formally, you can still become an exemplary leader by first leading yourself in achieving your goals. When you take charge and make things happen you're setting an example for others. As former US President John Quincy Adams declared…

> *"If your actions inspire others to dream more, learn more, do more and become more, you're a leader."*

As you proactively take on increasing responsibilities, adopting more of a service-oriented I-really-care-about-people attitude, you grow as an exemplary leader. You have empathy for others and their challenges, and genuinely want to help them with what you have to offer or share, wholeheartedly applying yourself in doing so.

A servant-leadership attitude is at the core of being a happy exemplary leader, creating win-win relationships. It's the opposite of a begrudging it's-all-about-me attitude, which, unfortunately, far too many people seem to have. As you've probably noticed, those with a self-absorbed attitude are definitely *not* happy, no matter what they're doing or who they're doing it with…and nobody wins!

Since we all choose our attitudes and actions, and leaders lead by example, you're actually a leader in as much as your attitude and actions—good, bad, or indifferent—are examples to others. Since we're always observing each other to one degree or another, you may have a bigger influence on those around you than you might imagine. So what would you like them to observe about you and emulate?

Why Not Set the Example of Being a Happy Exemplary Leader?

Exemplary leaders are constantly reaching out to others, observing and recognizing the needs of the people they meet and doing the best they can to serve. Being generous of heart, they take the initiative in guiding, serving, and encouraging their prospects, customers, and associates. They support them in overcoming fears and objections, fulfilling quality product and service wants and needs, while offering solutions for reaching greater levels of health, beauty, well-being, success, and happiness.

An exemplary leader earnestly recommends that associates who want to build the business take full advantage of available resources for increasing product, service, opportunity, and business-building knowledge, as well as for growing themselves personally. They're dedicated to inspiring and empowering them in developing to where they can effectively emulate the exemplary leader.

Now you may be asking, "How can I be an exemplary leader to customers and prospects? Am I not simply to provide them with what they say they want?" While certain customers and prospects have a good sense of what they want or need, others may only *think* they know what will best suit. As a leader and shareperson, it's your responsibility to determine how you could best serve them.

However, a customer or prospect may well have an uneducated or preconceived notion of what you're sharing. If this weren't so, they wouldn't need your guidance, would they? But even if you're relatively new and inexperienced, you still know more than your prospects or customers, and otherwise have ready access to the information they want or need.

Since exemplary leaders go the "extra mile" in sincerely befriending and serving others, they have a greater chance of gaining new customers and associates as well as retaining current ones.

Exemplary Leaders Have a Life-Enhancing Impact on Others

As an exemplary leader, you're keenly aware of your responsibility to have a life-enhancing impact on others. Your strongly held values and principles provide a solid foundation for the actions you take, can have far-reaching effects on large numbers of people both within and outside your immediate sphere of influence. Your guidance and excellent example can serve as a catalyst for people to grow and cause your organization to rise to ever higher levels.

Your high moral standards will contribute to others in fortifying the traditional morality central to all success and happiness. Your unwavering principles can help unite your people in working together to pursue the goals and dreams that raise the quality of lives, as you fulfill the mission you've embraced for yourself, your people, and your organization as a whole.

Exemplary Leaders Evolve...They're Not Just Born That Way!

Most people don't set out to be leaders. But because of their willingness to express themselves openly, freely, and caringly, those who ardently want to can evolve from being good followers to exemplary leaders. They grow from the silent majority to the expressive minority. In following their purpose they do what's in their hearts to do, communicating and sharing what they have to offer, positively influencing others, making a difference in the process.

Growing as an exemplary leader is easier for those who have an unshakable winning attitude and are confident in and committed to working harder and smarter while helping others. The opportunities for exemplary leadership are everywhere for those who accept the responsibilities and challenges encountered along the way. You can't be an exemplary leader without taking on more responsibility and dealing with more challenges, as this comes with the territory. As Winston Churchill, former Prime Minister of England, pronounced during World War II...

"The price of greatness is responsibility."

Exemplary leaders build their associates' confidence by recognizing their winning qualities, and encourage them to eliminate any success-stealing habits. They show appreciation for what their people do and never disparage them for the skills they have yet to master, affirming their strengths rather than dwelling on their weaknesses. They promote self-belief and healthy self-esteem in others by helping them adopt positive expectations, recognizing them for what they already do well, and supporting them in developing other skills as needed.

But no matter how well developed we may be, everyone has weaknesses. Since no one's born an exemplary leader, give yourself and others time to grow, evolve, and succeed.

Exemplary Leaders Risk Making Mistakes and Failure!

Exemplary leaders don't live in fear! Anyone who does will stay stuck right where they are, preventing themselves from getting ahead. They'll never know what they could have accomplished had they simply gone forward in faith and taken on the greater responsibility necessary in working toward living their dream. Without mustering the courage to take risks no one can become an exemplary leader, make anything extraordinary happen, keep getting ahead and moving forward, or make the difference they'd love to make.

If we don't risk making mistakes or even failing, we'll never be able to overcome the fear of those two challenging "mentors." Yes, mentors! While it may not at first be obvious, their purpose is to help us learn what we need to in order to improve on what we're doing in developing ourselves as exemplary leaders.

While there's always some risk involved in doing something new or unfamiliar, it's just a normal part of growing and becoming an exemplary leader, and central to the excitement of being on the leading edge of brightening your future. This, then, further energizes you in mustering the courage to continue taking risks, as well as being an incentive to stretch and grow in rising above and beyond the average leader. As Ralph Waldo Emerson advised...

> *"Whatever course you decide upon there's always someone to tell you that you're wrong. There are always difficulties arising that tempt you to believe that your critics are right. To map out a course of action and follow it to the end requires...courage."*

If you make a mistake or fail at something, don't dwell on it. Learn from it and move on. Without the courage to risk you simply cannot grow into an exemplary leader, nor can you make your dreams and goals a reality. If you don't make decisions and take the actions necessary to get ahead, you'll fail by default! Anyone who's developed themselves as a principled person and exemplary leader has literally "failed" their way to success.

Exemplary leaders give others hope and knowledge when they share what they've learned from their experiences—victories and especially defeats, what worked, what didn't—as they faced adversity head-on and grew through the process. You'll learn your best leadership lessons from the experiences you gain by leading others, which often entails having the courage to risk making mistakes and failure.

Exemplary leaders are quite aware of what's happening and reflect on what's already happened ... so they can benefit from their mistakes and failures. While reflection is often neglected by budding leaders when things are going smoothly, this could lead to regret.

What About the Attitude..."If It Ain't Broke, Don't Fix It"?

This is a losing attitude. Things need to be "fixed" or maintained so they *don't* break! People need to keep learning and growing to prevent their spirits from "breaking." Encouraging them to do so is not only kind, but also good for the business generated by associate activity and retention. Constantly care about and inspire your people to take charge and make it happen…so they never even think about giving up. Everyone needs to hear that they can do it!

How about this as a winning attitude for exemplary leaders?

> *"Help everyone maintain winning spirits so they don't 'break,' sharing your winning attitude while encouraging them to learn, grow, and become the person they were created to be!"*

Average-thinking people tend to dwell on past negative results, remembering them longer and stronger than positive results, slowing or halting any progress they could make. Exemplary leaders avoid getting bogged down in negative circumstances, never allowing them to upset their winning attitude. Instead, they analyze and learn from them and move on, teaching their people to do the same.

Is Your Dream BIG Enough for You to Be an Exemplary Leader?

Having a BIG dream or objective is essential for becoming an exemplary leader. Only those who know where they're going and maintain a fervent desire for it will take charge and make it happen, overcoming whatever obstacles they encounter. They're passionate about living their purpose, fulfilling their mission, guided by a vision for a brighter future for themselves and their family, as well as for those they lead and serve.

Couple all of this with the relentless focus needed for consistent progress and you can build the momentum to expand business as you become the exemplary leader you want to be. Be ever confident, uplifting, kind, and caring toward others, whether their dream, objective, or desire is big or small, and maintain a good sense of humor.

As you pursue your BIG dream, always be considerate of others; never pushy. Remember, "You can't push a rope, but you can gently pull a wet noodle." Treat people as if they were wet noodles (sensitive) that can be gently pulled (led) and you won't alienate them.

Exemplary Leaders and the Trust Factor

Exemplary leaders have exemplary character, and are congruent in their vision and actions. They gain and sustain trust, saying what they mean and meaning what they say. If they err, they take responsibility and apologize, clarify, and rectify the situation, as appropriate. They can be depended on for great guidance and encouragement.

Above all, exemplary leaders have integrity beyond reproach. They keep their promises even in the face of adversity, mistakes, circumstances, and failures. Integrity is strict adherence to a code of values like sincerity, honesty, and trustworthiness. Who would want to follow someone who couldn't be trusted or relied on?

If you talk about your vision and mission but don't follow through, or your actions result only in short-term or minimum results, your integrity will be diminished. People will be hesitant to believe what you say and less inclined to follow your lead. You would need to earn their trust back with committed follow through.

Exemplary Leaders Let People Know that They Matter

Exemplary leaders understand people and human nature. They respect everyone as a unique individual, and are generous in making as many people as possible aware of how they could benefit from what they have to offer. They realize effective communication occurs only when they reach out on the other person's level of reception, looking at them as if they have "WII-FM?" (What's In It—For Me?) printed on their foreheads. Therefore, "broadcast" your message on "radio station" WII-FM so people can receive it.

Exemplary leaders also look at people as if they have MMFI (Make Me Feel Important) printed on their shirt. Let people know they're important, that they matter to you, by what you say and how you treat them, and they'll be more inclined to listen and follow you.

Exemplary Leaders Attract and Develop Exemplary Leaders

Exemplary leaders are more likely to attract people with the qualities we so admire, better enabling their organization to grow and prosper for everyone's benefit. To more readily attract and develop exemplary leaders, you first need to at least be growing as one yourself! After all, people who are serious about getting ahead in life want to follow someone who's moving on and can help or guide them in doing the same.

You can develop exemplary leaders by emulating the exemplary leader who's been coaching you...offering your protégés appropriately earned leadership responsibilities when they're qualified... considering the specifics of your particular business. Encourage them to risk going forward, while accepting mistakes and failures as opportunities to learn, grow, and fine-tune what they're doing.

Never put anyone down for making an honest mistake. Instead, guide them in reviewing and correcting the situation as appropriate. Sincere empathy and encouragement assures budding leaders that mistakes are simply part of learning and growing as a leader.

Effects of Exemplary Leadership

When you lead people correctly and completely as an exemplary leader, your budding exemplary leaders will develop the 25 key attributes presented earlier in the chapter, guiding them to...

- Not live in the fear of failure or of making mistakes.
- Have the courage to risk moving forward.
- Bolster character, integrity, faith, wisdom, and solid values.
- Consistently be enthusiastic, day in and day out.
- Understand what causes them to have good "luck." As you'll recall, LUCK can be thought of as an acronym for ... Leadership, Understanding, Communication, and Knowledge.
- Have a vision and purpose that supports a mission which becomes central to all they do in their business or career, as well as in life.
- Regard change as a golden opportunity for growth.
- Not take themselves too seriously and have a good sense of humor.

Exemplary Leaders Support Others in Becoming All They Were Meant to Be, the Heart of True Success, Happiness, and Meaning

As a growing exemplary leader you'll be responsible for many things, the most decisive being your attitude! Maintain a humble winning attitude in all facets of who you are and what you're doing. This will enable you to overcome any shortcomings you may have, while setting the example for leading, helping, and serving others.

Since the world is suffused in negativity, think in positive winning ways for yourself, those you lead and serve, and all who could be affected by your attitude. Realizing your exemplary leadership can be the catalyst for countless others to get ahead and live a better life helps you persist and feel good about your mission as you grow and become all you were meant to be.

Your dedication to helping others, along with your unwavering commitment to the highest principles and values, will light the way for those who now live in the frustration and unhappiness of an everyday ordinary status-quo life. You have the opportunity, as well as the responsibility, to care about, encourage, and empower others for greater growth and accomplishment...as you inspire them with your exemplary leadership to be all they were meant to be, mutually finding the true success, happiness, and meaning everyone yearns for.

Seize the Opportunity…

Take charge and make it happen!

About Barnes Williamson

Barnes was a devoted husband and family man, who willingly and honorably served his country. After graduating from college, he held two sales positions before starting and building a successful career with a major insurance company.

As an agent, sales manager, and then agency leader, he received a President's Citation for every position he held, while earning over 55 awards for excellence in sales and leadership.

Active in professional, civic, and church affairs, he was president of two local trade associations, a member of two civic organizations, and served as an elder and clerk in his church. He was also on the board of directors and served as campaign chairman and chief volunteer officer of a local charity.

Barnes appeared on TV and radio talk shows and was the featured speaker at various civic and business organizations including the members and donors of his local YMCA, and at a leading financial services organization at their annual meeting.

Acknowledgment and the Publisher's Hope for You!

First of all, Barnes truly appreciated his positive, enthusiastic, always cheerful wife who made many sacrifices during his years of leading an insurance agency and in his research and writing.

He treasured his two daughters who painstakingly deciphered his writings and typed the original manuscript.

He valued the encouragement for this work that came from many friends, professional associates, community coworkers, and his church. He was thankful to all for their inspiration and wisdom.

He was thankful for his many mentors who helped him raise his attitude, optimism, and enthusiasm.

He was grateful for the knowledge, wisdom, and guidance of his editors and publisher for making this book possible, and everyone on the staff who contributed to making it what it developed into.

Last, but certainly not least, he thanked God for the opportunity of sharing this information to inspire and encourage others to take charge and make it happen...and, in turn, continue the sharing.

May this book be part of the worthy legacy of a highly accomplished, yet humble, man who passed away at 91 before we could publish it. By eliminating the stress he had allowed to develop in his early 60s and changing his health habits, Barnes continued living a great life that lasted over 30 years beyond his heart attack!

May the life-changing knowledge and wisdom presented in the book inspire and encourage you ... and those you share it with ... to develop a winning attitude, grow as a leader, and succeed by helping others.